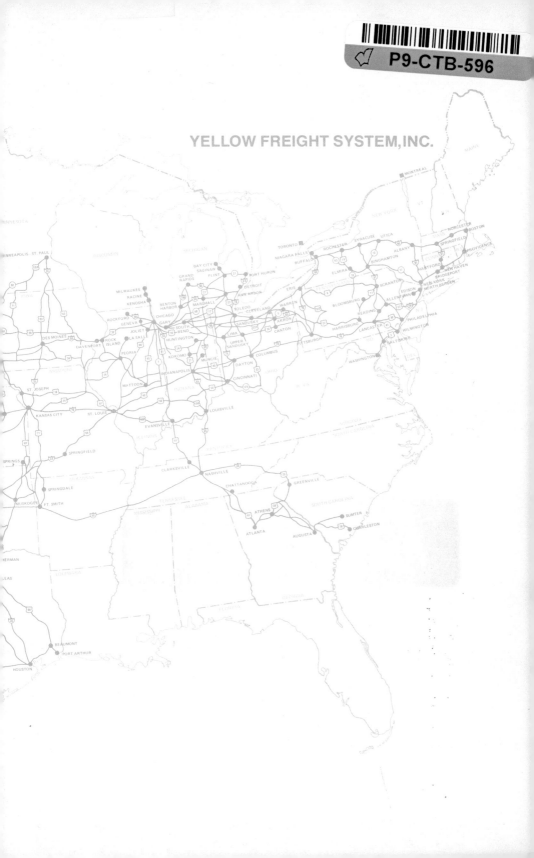

YELLOW FREIGHT SYSTEM, INC.

YELLOW IN MOTION

a history of
Yellow Freight System,
Incorporated

YELLOW IN MOTION

a history of
Yellow Freight System,
Incorporated

James F. Filgas

Indiana Business Report No. 41

Published by the School of Business
Division of Research/Indiana University

Cover design by DAVID NOBLETT

ACKNOWLEDGMENTS

During the preparation of this history, the facilities, personnel, and records of the Yellow Transit Freight Lines were completely and freely available to me. Mr. and Mrs. George Powell, Jr., Donald McMorris, and Mark Robeson spent many hours discussing company policies and history. Additional material was gained from a tour of the Texas terminals, expertly staged by Burl Cotton, and at a convention of the Associated Motor Carriers of Oklahoma at which Ray Alderson was my host. David Padgett, W. R. Riley, Harold Edwards, Connie Hale, L. E. Tomlinson, Lloyd Brandt, and their staffs were always ready to provide information and answers.

My research was further facilitated by William Glenn, who arranged research space and uncovered many valuable documents, and Kenneth Midgley, who opened his law office records for my perusal. The personnel at the Kansas City terminal answered the questions of the novice observer, and driver J. J. McNamara chauffeured me from Kansas City to Baxter Springs in a White Freightliner, and back in a "Jimmy Smoker." I also wish to thank W. L. Stevenson, longtime secretary to A. J. Harrell, for his hospitality and for relating the early history of the company.

Through all stages of research and preparation of the manuscript, I was assisted by L. L. Waters, University Professor of Transportation and Business History, Ross M. Robertson, chairman and professor of Business Economics and Public Policy and director of Business History Studies, and Joseph R. Hartley, associate dean of faculties, Indiana University. Editorial functions were performed by the editorial staff of the Bureau of Business Research. Finally, my parents Mr. and Mrs. John R. Filgas of Greenville, Mich. and Ellenton, Fla. provided office, home, and push throughout.

Preparing the revised edition was a refreshing experience. The people of the Yellow Freight System were very cooperative during the entire revision process. Mr. and Mrs. George Powell, Jr. and Dr. L. L. Waters were particularly helpful in the preparation of this edition.

JAMES F. FILGAS

Contents

Tables

ix

Photographs

Figures

INTRODUCTION

Transportation is a unique area of study and labor. Sometimes I think it is an incurable disease though not fatal. Men and women who fall victim cannot be happy in other gainful pursuits unless they find relief as an avocation. Thus, the railroads have almost as many "buffs" as employees. Bookshelves sag with thousands of volumes on every aspect of railroads, past and present. Other modes of transport have dedicated and "locked in" employees but have never developed *aficionados* of prose and song.

No great number of scholarly books is needed to accord the proper role to transport by means of motor carriers, pipelines, airlines, and barges. Yet a few are absolutely essential to give perspective to the functioning of our economy. This volume is only the third history and analysis of a trucking company in an industry that moves almost one-fourth of all ton-miles in the country for almost one-half of the transport revenue. The first volume, *Trucks, Troubles, and Triumph*, by Wayne Broehl, was published by Indiana University almost fifteen years ago. The second emerged elsewhere a few years later. This third should be the twentieth by this time.

We are pleased to release the current volume for its absolute value as a history of a particular company, for its superb lessons in corporate management, and, finally, as another of several components which must be written if subsequent business and economic historians are to write general, interpretive documents.

—L. L. Waters
University Professor of
Transportation and Business History

Executive Office Building, Yellow Transit Freight System, Inc.
92nd at State Line, Kansas City, Mo.

1 / ORIGINS OF YELLOW TRANSIT FREIGHT SYSTEM, INCORPORATED

The American business scene has provided many examples of business leaders who have shifted their managerial talents from one field to another. Some of the moves have occurred in a logical progression as the economy has expanded and changed; others have been made without apparent connection between the experiences of the businessmen involved. In the latter cases, success or failure can often be attributed to the ability to apply sound management principles to a variety of operational areas.

The history of Yellow Transit Freight System, Incorporated contains periods of each of these possibilities. The founder moved in logical steps from a livery barn to a truckline, the Yellow Transit Company. During another era, leaders from nonrelated fields moved to trucking without success from the then named Yellow Transit Freight Lines, Incorporated. In the final period, executives without trucking experience took over the company and, with management by logic, turned the line into an industry leader. In 1952, Yellow Transit was a "has-been" truckline floundering in the care of the bankruptcy court. A new management group saw possibilities, purchased the remains of the line, and went to work.

Complete understanding of the development of Yellow Freight System, Incorporated, the official corporate title since 1968, requires a knowledge of its history, beginning in Oklahoma City during the mid-1920's. The history can be divided into three distinct periods. During the first period, 1924-44, A. J. Harrell, the founder-owner, and his vice-president Evans A. Nash operated the line together. This was an era of struggle, growth, and profit. During the second period,

1

1944-52, Yellow Transit at first continued to advance, but, in the last two years, virtually collapsed. The company had ceased to be a single owner-operator truckline and was instead owned by a group of New York City investors. The third period spans the activity of the management group in control since 1952.

For several reasons, Yellow Transit Freight Lines merits careful study. First, of the thousands of trucklines founded since the advent of the motor vehicle, it is one of relatively few to survive—an achievement in itself. Second, the field of trucking has been relatively neglected as far as business history is concerned, and a study of this nature can add significantly to the literature. Yellow Freight System is an interesting choice for study because of its three-stage development from proprietorship to a closely held corporation and, finally, to its position as a publicly held corporation. The procedures and policies of a single company can be surprisingly different, depending on the goals and purposes of management and the area to be maximized— profit, personal gain, service, or perhaps size itself. Third, the trucking industry has been regarded by some as not quite as respectable as some other endeavors. By studying the personality of one unit within the industry insight on this notion may be gained.

Any company operates within the framework of its industry; in this study, care will be taken to relate how the workings of the firm were related to the entire industry. The contributions of Yellow Transit to trucking indicate that the firm has not been merely an impersonal, giant corporation but has been a company closely involved with the benefits of its employees and the advancement of the transportation industry.

THE EARLY YEARS

In 1904, an Illinois farm boy arrived in the territorial capital of Oklahoma City; this newcomer, A. J. Harrell, was to make a substantial contribution to the motor-carrier industry and to the economy of Oklahoma. Harrell was reared on a farm until he was about fourteen years old. Then, about 1895, his father "horse-traded" the farm for a livery barn at Olney, Ill.

The livery barn at Olney was operated by the Harrells until 1903. By that time, the younger Harrell had accumulated some finances of

A. J. Harrell

his own and went off to the St. Louis World's Fair where he met and joined two young men from Ohio on their way to see the country. One of the stops on the way west was Oklahoma City. Harrell liked the area and took a job selling buggies made by the Hercules Company of Evansville, Ind. The buggies cost the Oklahoma City dealer $35 each and sold for $85. Since they were shipped in lots of thirty-five, a reasonably large investment of $1,225 was required to purchase an inventory, but the return was also high. Apparently Harrell was a first-class salesman; in a short time, he had saved some money and was able to leave the job to go into the horse-and-mule business with an E. Bourne. This was a booming trade in the rapidly expanding Oklahoma Territory. Oil fields needed the animals for hauling, and Harrell quickly became knowledgeable in oil-field transportation requirements. Bourne, though a shrewd horse trader, was incapable of writing much more than his name, so all the paper work fell to Harrell, who acquired considerable experience in bookkeeping and oil-field equipment problems.

By 1921, the post-World War I lull in the national economy had hit the horse-and-mule business in Oklahoma, and, as a result, Harrell joined his brother, G. C. "Cleve" Harrell, who had started a taxi service, the Yellow Cab Company of Oklahoma City. The new business needed additional capital and manpower. Since taxicabs were shipped in lots of three per freight car to save freight costs, the Harrells acquired three at a time, at an average of one per month. When the fleet reached eighty-five, Yellow Cab was able to introduce "call stations." Cabs were based at several locations, thereby increasing flexibility, substantially decreasing gasoline consumption, tire wear, and so forth, and also reducing repairs and thus downtime.

During the mid-twenties, streetcar service from Oklahoma City to the Capitol Hill area was unreliable. Consequently, jitney operators began to serve the area. Their standard procedure was to charge according to ability to pay as they perceived it, and the result was lack of uniformity of rates. A. J. Harrell observed the growing demand for public transportation between the two points and presented to the city fathers a plan for bus service between Grand Avenue and Twenty-ninth Street that would both improve service and stabilize rates. The city granted Harrell a franchise for the bus operation, and he incorporated the business on Dec. 31, 1924 as the Yellow Cab Transit Company. The first entry in the corporation minutes book, on Jan. 1, 1925, reads as follows:

Capital stock	$250,000
Subscribers: G. C. Harrell	124 shares
A. J. Harrell	124 shares
Mae Harrell	1 share
Josie Harrell	1 share
Salary of president (G. C. Harrell)	$ 6,000
Salary of secretary (A. J. Harrell)	$ 6,000

A. J. Harrell had calculated correctly. Demand for the new bus service was brisk, and the Yellow Cab Transit Company bus operation prospered. Equipment consisted of Reo buses with a twenty-one passenger capacity. Eventually, eleven buses operated on the route. The schedule was a fifteen-minute run on a regular basis. The Harrells considered reliability particularly important, and the bus line attracted passengers from the trolley service offered by the Oklahoma Railway Company, which soon began negotiating to purchase the bus operation. After extended bargaining, the Harrells were offered what they considered a good price, and on March 31, 1926, the route franchise and equipment were sold.

During the time of the Oklahoma City-Capitol Hill bus operation, the buses and the fleet of Yellow cabs were using considerable quantities of gasoline. The Harrells studied several schemes in an attempt to reduce fuel costs and settled on a plan to integrate vertically. They opened a string of independent retail gasoline stations marketing Yellow Cab gasoline. The brand name was their own, of course, but their sources of supply were many. These ranged from several of A. J. Harrell's associates in his horse-and-mule-selling era to Phillips Petroleum Company. Eighteen stations were located in the Oklahoma City area. Not only was the retail gasoline business successful in its own right, but the Harrells were also able to supply fuel, grease, and oil for their cabs and buses at a substantial reduction.

After the sale of the local bus operation, the Yellow Cab Transit Company moved into the intercity bus business. The Harrells bought up several short permits and tied them together. They estimated that the total cost of this plan would be less, and, moreover, would allow them growing time. The first leg was from Oklahoma City east to Chandler, a distance of just under fifty miles. Next, the Chandler-Bristol run was acquired, adding thirty-odd miles. Then, a permit for the twenty-five miles from Bristol to Sapulpa was purchased. Sapulpa was connected with Tulsa by a rail transit company, and Yellow Cab Transit Company went through legal proceedings to acquire a permit for the final portion of the Oklahoma City-Tulsa trip. Eventually, the permit was granted, and Yellow Cab Transit possessed an operating permit for service between the two largest cities in Oklahoma—a distance of about 115 miles. It had taken more than a year to piece together the Oklahoma City-Tulsa operating authority.

The first intercity vehicles used were automobiles expanded to fourteen-passenger buses running approximately six schedules per day in each direction. Because the trade was heavy, two trailer-type buses mounted on White tractors—each capable of carrying thirty-two passengers—were added. The volume of business plus the strategic nature of the permit made the Yellow Cab Transit Company operation quite valuable, particularly to the Pickwick Stages, operating out of both Oklahoma City and Tulsa but not between. After extensive bargaining, the Yellow Cab Transit Company sold the Tulsa-Oklahoma City bus authority for $150,000 to the Pickwick Greyhound Lines, Incorporated. The deal was consummated on Aug. 23, 1929, but included was a provision that the Harrells would continue to operate the buses for an additional three months. The equipment exchanged in the transaction was listed as follows in the corporate minutes of Aug. 23, 1929:

Make	Seating Capacity	Purchase Date
Buick	7	April 27, 1928
Buick	7	Jan. 2, 1929
Yellow	20	July 6, 1927
Yellow	20	July 6, 1927
Yellow	20	July 6, 1927
Yellow	20	Aug. 1, 1927
Yellow	20	Aug. 1, 1927
Studebaker	18	May 5, 1928
Studebaker	18	May 5, 1928
Studebaker	18	May 31, 1928
Studebaker	18	May 31, 1928
Studebaker	14	May 31, 1928
White	32	April 25, 1929
White	32	April 25, 1929

In 1926, several motor carriers, including Reliable Truck Lines, Luper Transportation Company, and Clinton Truck Lines, were operating in the Oklahoma City area. The carriers needed a terminal, however, and A. J. Harrell therefore opened a consolidated motor freight terminal at Santa Fe and California Streets. Harrell had been eyeing the trucking business for some time, and he now had the opportunity to study firsthand what was being hauled, by whom, for whom, and where it was going.

In conjunction with the consolidated terminal, a pair of four-cylinder White trucks with straight truck bodies was purchased for use in local hauling. Harrell then approached the Oklahoma Corporation Commission and requested a permit to operate a truckline between Oklahoma City and Tulsa. Since Harrell enjoyed the prime requisite for permit securing in those days—friends on the commission—the authority was soon granted, and Yellow Cab Transit Company was in the intercity trucking business. The two White trucks were still in use in 1944, and their purchase might well be considered the actual beginning of Yellow Transit Freight Lines.[1]

EARLY TRUCKING OPERATIONS

The earliest trucking operations of the Yellow Cab Transit Company were inauspicious. Limited to only two vehicles, the company also had

[1]The material for this section relies heavily upon notes prepared by William H. Glenn, purchasing agent of Yellow Transit Freight Lines, following interviews with A. J. Harrell and Evans A. Nash at Oklahoma City on Jan. 9-10, 1958, and upon notes taken by the author during an interview with W. L. Stevenson, longtime secretary to Harrell, at Oklahoma City on Oct. 31, 1963.

The Original Yellow Transit Company Fleet

to compete for managerial attention with the bus line, taxicab, and terminal endeavors. The Harrells were also engaged in oil and cattle interests in the state. In all these businesses, the Harrells took an active managerial role; they were not passive investors.

Nevertheless, trucking held particular fascination for A. J. Harrell, and in late 1929, particularly after the sale of the Oklahoma City-Tulsa bus line, he began pushing the trucking business. The decision to operate the truckline over the route of the Yellow Cab Transit bus line was based on the fact that such a move connected the largest commercial centers of the state.

Oklahoma City and Tulsa were booming oil towns during the 1920's. Population grew during this decade from 91,295 to 185,389 in Oklahoma City, and from 72,075 to 141,258 in Tulsa. As might be expected, the first substantial cargo of the freight line was parts and equipment for the drilling and pumping of oil. Harrell's earlier experience with oil-field operators during his horse-and-mule-selling days doubtless provided the first list of potential customers. A second source of customers for the truckline developed from the bus operations. The buses served as freight-haulers, also, with some shippers using the Yellow Cab Transit Company buses for express freight moving. The early schedules of the Yellow Transit trucks were fast and "bus-like" to capture this trade.

The trucking operations were not an immediate financial success. A Jan. 1, 1929 entry in the company minutes reads as follows: "Because of the improvement of the company's [sic] and the fact that a great deal of time is being consumed in managing the company's business, the stockholders authorized the payment of a salary of $6,000.00 per year to each the President and Secretary beginning January 1, 1929." (In 1928, the salaries had been $3,600.) And a year later, the minute book entry recorded the following: "It was explained that because of the opening of a freight-line business, the funds of the company were low and would continue so until the new business had been established." On the same day, A. J. Harrell was elected president for 1930, and he was to serve without a salary. The company was indeed fortunate to have owner-officers financially able to forgo salaries when times were slow.

The Harrell interests at that time still included several operations: taxicabs, the consolidated truck terminal, the retail gasoline stations, the new freight line, and, until November, 1929, the Oklahoma City-Tulsa bus operation. If a breakdown of the finances of the many endeavors was then maintained, it is no longer in existence; thus, a recorded figure of the truckline's success or failure is not available. However, company files reveal that during the first three months of operation the truckline lost $18,000. This period was probably October, November, and December, 1929, since the Oklahoma Corporation Commission granted approval of the operation on Sept. 6, 1929. The operation of the truckline was reported profitable thereafter. The first statement found for the separate operation of the truckline indicates a net income of $32,290.32 for 1931. The income was gained on revenues of $231,472.76, making net income 13.9 per cent of revenue.[2]

By 1931, the freight operation had been separated from the other business ventures of the Harrell brothers. Separate records were maintained for the truckline, which retained the corporate name of Yellow Cab Transit Company, but which did business as the Yellow Transit Company. The freight business had become a dominant part of the Harrell enterprises, and separation enabled the owners to concentrate on route expansion.

The two initial expansions of Yellow Transit Company's truckline were north to Kansas City and south to Dallas. The move north from

---

[2]Evans A. Nash & Co., Accountants & Auditors, "Report of Audit, Yellow Cab Transit Company," Dec. 31, 1931.

Tulsa to Baxter Springs, Kan., Joplin, Mo., and Kansas City was made because A. J. Harrell had observed the large amount of interchange traffic received at Tulsa from these places. Baxter Springs and Joplin were also interchange points, with the bulk of traffic arriving from distant points by some other carrier. Kansas City, on the other hand, was a large freight origination center. This segment of the Yellow Transit route was added by requesting original operating authority, which the state of Kansas granted on Aug. 30, 1930. The Oklahoma City-Dallas portion came into the Yellow Transit operational area when A. J. Harrell purchased an existing line, which was in financial distress. Harrell used his trading experience to advantage in this transaction and bought the line for little more than the attorney's fees—about $600 or $700.

The extension into Texas presented Yellow Transit with a minimum-weight problem. Trucks entering Texas at the Red River were limited to 7,000-pound loads. Since Oklahoma's load limit at that time was at least three times as much, a 21,000-pound load had to be broken into three parts for the journey south of the Texas border. For several years Yellow Transit maintained a terminal at Thackerville, Okla., close to the border, for breaking purposes.

On June 26, 1931, the board of directors of the Yellow Transit Company authorized the extension of the company's operation into Houston. This move, like the one into Dallas, was accomplished by purchasing an in-debt carrier. This leg of the expanding Yellow Transit routes was the first balanced portion, with northbound traffic approximately equaling the southbound flow. Such balance is highly desirable, of course, because equipment utilization can be maximized more readily when the flow of tonnage is about the same both ways over a given run. (The 1931 routes from Kansas City to Tulsa, Tulsa to Dallas, and Dallas to Houston are depicted in Figure 1.)

The next expansion move was into St. Louis; Yellow Transit purchased the rights of the Selby Motor Freight Lines along U.S. Highway 66 from Joplin through Springfield and Rolla to St. Louis. The Selby Lines, founded as Banner Truck Lines, Incorporated, became Selby Motor Freight on Jan. 7, 1935. Inclusion in the Yellow Transit family came on Sept. 4, 1935, when the name was again changed to Yellow Cab Transit Company of Missouri. The Missouri company remained separate from the parent company until merger of the two was approved by the Interstate Commerce Commission on Sept. 19, 1939. Directors of the Missouri company were A. J. Harrell, Evans A. Nash,

FIGURE 1

Yellow Transit Expansions, 1931

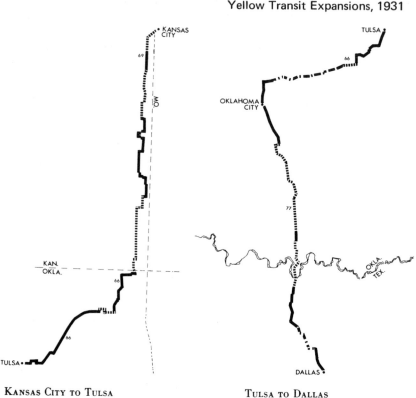

KANSAS CITY TO TULSA   TULSA TO DALLAS

M. M. Harrell, and James T. Blair, Jr., who was later elected governor of Missouri.

The Yellow Transit system of lines was developed to this point when the company filed its "grandfather clause" application with the ICC on Jan. 9, 1936 for a certificate of public convenience and necessity. The exact routes requested were:

1. Between Kansas City, Missouri, and Houston, Texas, over U.S. Highway 69 from Kansas City to Baxter Springs, Kansas, U.S. Highway 66, thence to Oklahoma City, Oklahoma, U.S. Highway 77, thence to Dallas, Texas, and U.S. Highway 75, thence to Houston.

2. Between Denton and Longview, Texas, over U.S. Highway 377 from Denton to Fort Worth, Texas, U.S. Highway 80, thence via Dallas to Mineola,

DALLAS

75

PAVED ROADS, concrete, brick,
macadam, asphalt

IMPROVED ROADS, gravel,
stone, shell, sand, clay

75

GRADED ROADS, smooth and
drained dirt

HOUSTON

DALLAS TO HOUSTON

Texas, U.S. Highway 69, thence to Tyler, Texas, U.S. Highway 271, thence to
Gradewater, Texas, and U.S. Highway 80, thence to Longview.

3. Between St. Louis, Missouri, and Houston, via Baxter Springs and Route
1, thence to Houston.

4. Between Kansas City and Houston via Baxter Springs, Vinita, and Atoka,
Oklahoma, Denison and Dallas, Texas, and Route 1, thence to Houston.

5. Between St. Louis and Houston via Baxter Springs and Route 4, thence
to Houston.

6. Between Tulsa, Oklahoma, and Houston via Muskogee and Route 4,
thence to Houston.

7. Between Kansas City and Houston via Fort Scott, Wichita, Wellington,
and Hunnewell, Kansas, Perry and Oklahoma City, Oklahoma, and Route 1,

thence to Houston; with an alternate route from Wellington via Winfield and
Arkansas City, Kansas, and Ponca City, Oklahoma, to U.S. Highway 77.[3]

Division 5 of the commission decided on July 29, 1938, however,
that Route 2 was justified only between Denton and Dallas. In addition,
the "short route" via Vinita and Atoka, Okla. in Routes 4, 5, and 6
was disallowed. On Sept. 6, 1939, Yellow Transit requested operating
authority over the rejected short route via U.S. Highway 69, and on
July 3, 1941, the commission approved the request. Yellow Transit
submitted testimony claiming a saving of $34,000 per year as a result
of the 180-mile reduction in distance per round trip between Baxter
Springs and Dallas.

The grandfather clause application was submitted under the Motor
Carrier Act approved by President Franklin D. Roosevelt on Aug. 9,
1935. This clause provided that certificates of public convenience and
necessity were to be granted to carriers in bona fide operation at the
time of the passage of the act. June 1, 1935 was the critical date for
common carriers such as Yellow Transit. The ICC interpreted the act
rather strictly in an effort to prevent the granting of operating authority
more extensive than that actually exercised by the applying carrier. In
disallowing some of Yellow Transit's route mileage, the ICC held that
the company had not regularly utilized those routes in carrying out its
scheduled truck operations. The Yellow Transit application was one of
75,977 grandfather clause cases the commission had received by Feb.
12, 1936.[4]

ENDERS AND BRYAN ADDED

Before the outcome of this application was known, Yellow Transit
embarked on its next growth plan. On July 27, 1937, the company
submitted to the commission a plan for the purchase of the H. H.
Enders Truck Line. Four years later, on July 3, 1941, the commission
decided in favor of the purchase. Through the operating rights of this
company, Yellow Transit succeeded in gaining entrance to San An-

[3]Interstate Commerce Commission, "Yellow Cab Transit Company Common Carrier Application," *Reports, Motor Carrier Cases*, VIII (Washington: U.S. Gov't
Printing Office), pp. 279-82.

[4]Although many figures are cited for the number of these cases, the ICC's own
figure is used here. Interstate Commerce Commission, *Annual Report, 1936* (Washington: U.S. Gov't Printing Office), p. 70.

tonio. The Enders line had operated between Enid, Okla. and San Antonio with coverage of Wichita Falls and Bowie, Tex. An additional route between San Antonio and Beaumont through Houston via U.S. Highway 90 was also acquired. The agreed-upon purchase price of the Enders company was $12,500.

One of the largest expansions of the Yellow Transit system came about through a merger with the Bryan Motor Freight Lines, Incorporated. This carrier possessed operating rights of 1,382 miles and covered the area from Kansas City to Amarillo, Tex. The specific routes were from Tulsa to Amarillo, via U.S. Highway 66; McLean to Pampa, Tex.; Tulsa to Wichita; Oklahoma City to Kansas City, Mo., via Wichita and Emporia, Kan.; and between Wichita and Kansas City, via Salina, Kan. The Bryan lines were acquired by A. J. Harrell as a personal investment on Aug. 11, 1936 for $18,000. The owner of Bryan Motor Freight was anxious to sell for health reasons, and Harrell considered $18,000 a bargain price. Because he could not convince the company to buy it, he bought and ran the Bryan company separately until merger was approved by the ICC on March 7, 1939. Complete dissolution of the Bryan company occurred on Dec. 22, 1939 by action of the Texas Secretary of State. The ICC stated in the merger proceedings that "there appears to be little justification for continued separate corporate existence of Yellow Cab and Bryan under common control, in view of the substantial route duplications."[5]

At the time of merger in 1939, Yellow Transit acquired some $44,-051 worth of equipment with accrued depreciation of $23,581. The equipment consisted of one 1938 Ford gasoline truck, one 1936 International gasoline truck, six 1936 International gasoline tractors, seven 1937 International gasoline tractors, six 1933 Mack gasoline tractors, six 1936 Fruehauf trailers, and seven 1937 Fruehauf trailers.

Since the Bryan lines had been owned by Harrell, the policies regarding equipment had been the same, and Yellow Transit had only to paint new signs to incorporate the former Bryan fleet.

Statistics from Bryan's annual reports to the ICC indicate that operating revenues totaled $148,354 during 1938 and $121,810 for the time Bryan was operated separately in 1939. Operating expenses for the same

[5]Interstate Commerce Commission, "Yellow Cab Transit Company—Control—Bryan Motor Freight Lines, Incorporated; A. J. Harrell—Control—Yellow Cab Transit Company," *Reports, Motor Carrier Cases*, XV (Washington: U.S. Gov't Printing Office), pp. 770-72.

periods were $103,003 and $82,985, with net incomes of $11,323 for
1938 and $10,035 for part of 1939. Net income as a percentage of
revenues was 7.6 per cent for 1938 and 8.2 for 1939. The average
number of employees during this period was thirty-seven, and the 1938
payroll was $53,969. Average annual compensation for drivers and
helpers was $1,515; for terminal employees, $938; and for general
officers, $4,772. Total miles operated were 849,014 in 1938 and 692,-
208 in 1939. Total assets were listed as $54,635 at the close of 1938.
Bryan Motor Freight, at the outset a relatively small concern, had
prospered under Harrell.

Included in the application to combine the operations of Bryan
Motor Freight Lines with the Yellow Transit Company was a proposal
for absorption of the Yellow Cab Transit Company of Missouri. This
subsidiary had operated 315 miles of line via U.S. Highway 66 from
St. Louis to the Missouri-Kansas boundary near Baxter Springs. The
Missouri company, although operating but a few miles, possessed total
assets of $163,935 at the close of 1938. Of this figure, $117,834 was
classified in the ICC uniform system of accounts as "tangible property,"
with a further breakdown of $63,120 as revenue equipment: two 1936
Mack gasoline tractors, one 1936 Chevrolet gasoline tractor, eight 1937
Mack gasoline tractors, two 1934 Chevrolet gasoline trucks, one 1937
Ford gasoline truck, one 1938 Ford gasoline truck, eight 1935 Fruehauf
trailers, and seven 1938 Fruehauf trailers. The merger consolidated
all equipment and property formerly held by the Missouri company.

Of the 100 shares of stock of the Yellow Cab Transit Company of
Missouri, 99 were held by the shareholders of the Yellow Cab Transit
Company of Oklahoma. The single remaining share was in the name
of James T. Blair, Jr. as qualifying director's share in Missouri.

Operating revenues during the last two periods of independent operations of the Missouri company, according to their annual reports to
the ICC, were $217,871 for 1938 and $289,896 for 1939. The Missouri
company carried both intrastate and interstate cargo along its single
line through Missouri, but by far the largest portion of the business
was traffic moving from St. Louis or beyond to the Oklahoma and
Texas points served by Yellow Transit. Net income for the same two
periods was $24,685 and $38,104; net income as a percentage of gross
revenues was 11.3 per cent and 13.2 per cent. The Missouri company
had employed an average of fifty-two persons in 1938; during 1939
the number grew to seventy-six. The number of drivers and helpers
rose from thirteen to twenty-five, the largest share of the increase. The
average compensation per year during the 1938-39 period was $1,356

for drivers and helpers, $1,244 for terminal employees, and $3,032 for general officers. Mileage covered in intercity truck service in 1938 was 1,008,671; this figure increased to 1,242,165 in 1939.

The power behind the suggestion to include the Missouri company in the Bryan merger proceeding was the ICC. Yellow Transit had wished to purchase the Kern Motor Express properties of Jesse W. Kern, and in a proceeding decided on June 7, 1939, the commission found that the purchase would be in the public interest if the Yellow Cab Transit Company of Missouri were brought into the fold as "connector." The commission noted that Kern operated from St. Louis east and that Yellow Transit routes extended from the Missouri-Kansas state line west and south—some 315 miles from St. Louis. The bridge carrier was the Missouri company, wholly owned by Yellow Transit, and the commission required that the Missouri company be merged with Yellow Transit. The specific statement of benefits to be realized was as follows:

> The merger proposed is in line with our policy to encourage corporate simplification, would bring an end to the undesirable operating situation discussed in Yellow Cab Transit Co.—Purchase—Kern, *supra*, and would simplify regulation under the act. Economies would be effected through elimination of separate tariffs, solicitation, advertising, accounting, and annual reports; tracing of shipments would be simplified; and service to the shipping public generally would be improved through rearrangements of schedules and elimination of present interchange.[6]

Kern Motor Express operated between Evansville, Ind. and St. Louis via Vincennes, Ind. and Salem, Ill. This route followed U.S. Highway 50 from Vincennes to St. Louis and passed through Olney, the birthplace of A. J. Harrell. In addition, Kern operated between Evansville and East St. Louis via New Harmony, Ind. and Mount Vernon and Belleville, Ill. and had a branch between Princeton and Winslow, Ind. The Kern purchase was completed with a cash payment of $8,000, which included the transfer to Yellow Transit of two trucks appraised at a total value of $1,000.

Oil-field development in central Illinois motivated the expansion into that area. Several oil-field supply companies had established ware-

---

[6]Interstate Commerce Commission, "Yellow Cab Transit Company (Oklahoma) —Merger—Bryan Motor Freight Lines, Incorporated, and Yellow Cab Transit Company (Missouri)," *Reports, Motor Carrier Cases*, XXV (Washington: U.S. Gov't Printing Office), pp. 545-46.

houses there, including those at Centralia, Salem, Clay City, and Cross-
ville. Kern Motor Express served each of these points, providing an
excellent addition to the Yellow Transit System. Harrell was assured
by friends in Oklahoma and Texas that the area, then just developing,
was certain to expand. Moreover, transportation of equipment from
manufacturers in the Texas area, such as the Hughes Tool Company at
Houston, would be long-haul business. Another feature of the oil-field
traffic was its northbound character. Yellow Transit has always had a
predominantly southward flow of traffic; this move helped balance the
flow, thereby eliminating some empty trailer movement. The ICC recognized this point in the following statement regarding the Kern purchase:

> By this purchase, applicant would acquire rights over routes serving the
> recently developed oil fields of southern Illinois and vicinity. It expects to
> participate in the movement of an increasing volume of oilwell equipment and
> supplies from Texas and Oklahoma points to that area, handling manufactured
> products in the reverse direction. By eliminating present interchange with
> vendor at St. Louis and the use of applicant's terminal at that point, overhead
> costs would be reduced, and schedules would be expedited from 6 to 12 hours.[7]

By late 1939, the Kern properties, the Bryan Motor Freight Lines,
and the Yellow Cab Transit Company of Missouri were all included in
the Yellow Cab Transit Company of Oklahoma (doing business as the
Yellow Transit Company). The company's lines now extended from
Evansville and Vincennes, Ind. in the north to Amarillo and Houston
in the Southwest. An additional route north from Dallas extended to
Kansas City and Wichita, and an application was pending for the purchase of the H. H. Enders Truck Line into San Antonio.

In 1938, the first year the ICC compiled statistics from annual reports,
Yellow Transit was one of 944 Class I (annual operating revenues in
excess of $100,000) intercity carriers. The wholly owned Bryan Motor
Freight and Yellow Cab Transit Company of Missouri properties also
were in this group, but the combined gross revenues of all three—just
over $1 million—were a small portion of total 1938 U.S. truckline
revenues of $310 million.

---

[7]Interstate Commerce Commission, "Yellow Cab Transit Company—Purchase—
Jesse W. Kern," *Reports, Motor Carrier Cases*, XXV (Washington: U.S. Gov't
Printing Office), pp. 264-66.

2 / POLICIES AND PROCEDURES OF A. J. HARRELL

In 1921, A. J. Harrell had joined his brother G. C. "Cleve" in operating the Yellow Cab Company of Oklahoma City. The two brothers eventually set up an equally owned business partnership—with diverse interests—known as Harrell Brothers, but by 1937 their interests had diverged to the point where dissolution of the partnership was necessary. An agreement was signed on May 10, 1937, and the assets of the partnership were divided.

The Yellow Cab Company of Oklahoma City and the chain of Yellow Cab gasoline stations were retained by G. C. Harrell; the oil and cattle interests went to his brother. Control of the major portion of the partnership, the Yellow Transit Company, required Interstate Commerce Commission approval, and the case was submitted to the ICC on Nov. 5, 1937. The following plan was approved on May 7, 1939. Yellow Transit Company had 2,500 authorized and outstanding shares of capital stock, par value $100 each. Before the May 10, 1937 agreement, the division of shares had been as follows: 1,165 shares owned by A. J. Harrell; 1,165 shares held by G. C. Harrell; 20 shares held by a third brother, M. M. Harrell; and 150 shares owned by Yellow Transit vice-president, Evans A. Nash. Under the May 10 agreement, A. J. Harrell was to purchase the 1,165 shares owned by his brother for $85,000 and his interest in certain partnership assets relating to Yellow Transit for approximately $140,000, or $120 per share. In approving the plan, the ICC noted:

For the past two years A. J. and G. C. Harrel have been unable to coordinate their views as to policies and general conduct of their motor-carrier and other business enterprises. Several attempts were made to adjust their differences in manner mutually agreeable, finally resulting in the dissolution agreement mentioned. Stock control of Yellow Cab by A. J. Harrell has eliminated internal strife, has had a stabilizing influence on operations, and has resulted in improved service.[1]

The commission further pointed out that "the record shows that A. J. Harrell had sufficient cash as of the hearing date to discharge the obligation to his brother . . . ."

The major disagreement seems to have been over the expansion of the Yellow Transit Company system. G. C. "Cleve" Harrell would not join in the purchase of the Bryan Motor Freight Lines in 1936, and A. J. personally bought Bryan's capital stock. The reasons for this division, which had such a profound effect on Yellow Transit, were based on personality differences between the two brothers and the policies and procedures adopted by A. J. Harrell and his employees.

PERSONALITIES

G. C. "Cleve" Harrell, an established businessman in the taxicab field in Oklahoma City when he enlisted his brother's aid, was apparently willing to take chances; otherwise, he would not have risked starting the taxicab service in frontier-like Oklahoma City. At the same time, however, he was quite satisfied to stay with a good thing. He apparently wanted to improve the cab company to the point where it could provide the highest quality service with maximum profits.

His brother, on the other hand, was more willing to take risks. He had been a buggy salesman, a horse-and-mule peddler, and a part-time bookkeeper, and had been engaged in several other odd jobs for short periods. He was always looking around for sound new business deals; he had an intercity bus line, established a consolidated freight terminal, which offered local cartage on the side, and started the intercity trucking business. He also possessed substantial oil and cattle interests. A. J. Harrell was certainly an adventurous man and an eager entrepreneur.

---

[1]Interstate Commerce Commission, "Yellow Cab Transit Company—Control—Bryan Motor Freight Lines, Incorporated; A. J. Harrell—Control—Yellow Cab Transit Company," *Reports, Motor Carrier Cases*, XV (Washington: U.S. Gov't Printing Office), pp. 769-72.

Both brothers admired quality workmanship, were willing to work hard for what they wanted, and exhibited independence of spirit and considerable initiative. These characteristics seem to have bound them together during their partnership. Essentially, the Harrell endeavors were pioneering efforts in untried businesses and in recently developed territory. Workers' initiative, trustworthiness, and inventiveness were considered more important than acquired skills or operational abilities. Therefore, men hired as taxi drivers, dock workers, and ranch hands were carefully screened. The first requirement was usually a personal interview with A. J. Harrell. He was a straight-speaking man, who told prospective employees precisely what he expected of them and what they, in turn, could expect of him. He was tough but willing to pay extra for quality. His idea was that by paying perhaps 5 per cent more he could expect about 10 per cent better work, and most of the time he was proven right. In addition, the Harrells always checked a man's past performance. A prison record was almost certain cause for rejection, and credit ratings were especially important to them; the Harrells maintained that a man who paid his bills fairly would work fairly.

The brothers were known for providing first-class equipment and excellent working conditions, hoping thereby to attract a superior work force. They managed to do so, at least in the trucking business, because Yellow Transit was noted for its good drivers from the beginning. A. J. Harrell liked big men for truck drivers and hired many former oil-field workers for his truckline. Their physical toughness was an asset in the early days of trucking; roads were usually unpaved, the job was demanding, and a husky driver was less likely to be hijacked. New drivers were on probation for about three months and spent some time with seasoned men before going out on their own. This was the Yellow Transit training system, and over the years the plan worked admirably.

POLICIES AND PROCEDURES

New Personnel

As the truckline grew, so did the need for specialized men, such as auditors, agents, rate men, and others experienced in transportation. A. J. Harrell, who was especially interested in the management of the truckline, met this challenge by hiring M. M. Harrell, a third brother, as secretary of the Yellow Transit Company. The new secretary had worked in railroad offices for twenty years and had many friends in the railroad industry. As a result, many of the developing office spots in the Yellow Transit Company were filled with ex-railroad men. Because Yellow Transit was one of the few growing concerns during the Great Depression, capable men were readily available at rather low salary levels. Many hired at that time became valuable employees holding important positions.

At the beginning, A. J. Harrell created the position of general manager as second in command. The first man to hold this job was described by Harrell as a "politician and capitol man" with good connections; he was discharged after three months, however, when he recommended that the business be sold. (Yellow Transit had lost $18,-000 during its first three months of operation.) For the next three years, 1930-32, Harrell employed an ex-railroader turned bus line manager; unfortunately, he saw no future for the company either.

In 1932, Evans A. Nash was hired as vice-president of Yellow Transit Company; this move was unquestionably the most significant personnel gain of the company during Harrell's ownership. Nash, born in St. Joseph, Mo., had a varied career before joining Yellow Transit. After his graduation from a small Kansas college, he was a newspaperman until he became an auditor in the state offices at Oklahoma City. Finding such work to his liking, Nash undertook the formal study of accounting, passed the examinations, and became a certified public accountant. About 1918, he joined in the formation of an accounting firm called Hammonds and Nash, which operated until Nash joined Yellow Transit. Harrell felt that Nash, who had been auditing the taxicab business on a monthly basis, was just the man needed as general manager. Although Nash lacked trucking experience, he was skilled in financial matters, and, in addition, he was convinced that A. J. Harrell was the man for whom he wanted to work. For the next twelve years, Nash was vice-president of Yellow Transit Company.

Harrell had made a wise choice; the new general manager was a businessman of the newer facts-and-figures, cost-conscious school. Indeed, within a month after joining Yellow Transit, Nash himself was completely convinced that he had a real role to perform in the area of financial management. At a trucking industry meeting in Kansas City, he discovered that most truck operators were self-established former drivers who lacked managerial talent in the area of investment decisions, budgeting, and money matters in general. Yellow Transit was fortunate to acquire a true financial manager some years before most other trucking companies.

Evans A. Nash

Harrell's Cash Policy

The policy for which A. J. Harrell gained the most notice was his cash-for-everything plan. On occasion, to keep the business on the cash plan, he would loan the company large sums from his personal estate. The rate of interest he charged the company was slightly under the commercial rate of the time, but Yellow Transit Company enjoyed a ready source of credit during a time when most trucklines had to beg for loans. Harrell felt that making the company save in advance would limit expenditures and investments to those really needed. This conservative policy was, in some way, his own capital budgeting procedure.

The cash policy applied to pencils as well as to real estate, an area in which the policy was remarkably effective. For example, in about 1935, Harrell wanted to acquire property for a terminal in Dallas. A real estate man lined up some fifteen sites, and Harrell went to Dallas to look them over. One piece of property looked ideal to him until he was told that the price was $94,000. Harrell thereupon called the president of the owning company, the Rock Island Plow Company, and offered $30,000. The president scoffed at the suggestion until Harrell quietly added the word "cash." The next morning the deal went through.

A second terminal location purchase occurred in Kansas City. Harrell looked over several possibilities and finally decided on a parcel of land owned by the St. Louis Casket Company. The tract was valued at over $54,000, but, by offering cash and a quick deal, Harrell received the title for $15,000.[2] These property exchanges, of course, were consummated during the Depression when cash was extremely scarce; perhaps Harrell's ability to command and protect liquid resources was more noteworthy than his real estate finesse.

Equipment purchases were also handled on a cash basis. On one occasion, Yellow Transit ordered forty-two Mack tractors; three a month were to be delivered for fourteen months. The payments were made on a thirty-sixty-ninety-day basis; thus, the tractors were in service and bringing in revenue before the first one-third was due. On that particular lot of Macks, Harrell figured that he saved $600 per tractor.

As would be expected, supplies and materials were also purchased for cash. In fact, both Harrell and Nash were strong advocates of the notion that all cash payments should be discounted, and this was the policy at the Yellow Transit Company for many years.

Terminals and Equipment

During the Harrell era, Yellow Transit built its own terminals; the designers were Harrell himself and his superintendent of construction. The superintendent took charge of the actual construction, but Harrell had much to say about how the terminals were to be set up. One of these buildings was the Oklahoma City terminal, built in 1938 on Western Avenue. The first floor was devoted to truck operations with dock space; the second floor housed the general offices of the Yellow Transit Company; and the third floor was a spacious penthouse apartment—the home of Mr. and Mrs. A. J. Harrell. In many ways, the early Yellow Transit Company was a one-man show, and the owner intended to be there for all performances.

Several other terminals in the Yellow Transit System also contained living quarters for the terminal manager and his family. Some of these were acquired when Yellow Transit purchased smaller lines that had been owner-operator companies; the owner had lived at the chief terminal just as Harrell did at Oklahoma City. Harrell encouraged this arrangement; not only was the manager available when needed, but his wife could act as secretary.

[2]"Yellow Transit 'Growing Since 1924 Through Serving Better'," *Transport Topics* (Oct. 20, 1958), p. 79.

The functional setup of the Yellow Transit System during this early period was on a divisional basis, with maintenance and repair garages at the center of the divisions. In 1932, Yellow Transit maintained garages at Oklahoma City, Kansas City, and Dallas. The Dallas garage served the Texas operations of the company, which amounted to the line from Thackerville, Okla., near the Texas boundary, to Houston. The divisional setup also followed weight restriction laws and operating characteristics to some extent. Since weight limitations in Texas were more severe, that area was singled out for special treatment. Smaller trucks, tractors, and trailers moved from the Thackerville breaking point into Texas; northbound loads were consolidated at Thackerville and moved out in larger equipment. The Dallas garage was geared to keep the lighter Texas equipment rolling in first-class condition. The Oklahoma City garage was the busiest of the three and serviced Oklahoma, the heart of company operations. The headquarters station also possessed specialized equipment required for larger jobs and unusual repairs and was the company's major repair station. A small Kansas City garage took care of problems on that end of the line.

Shortly after the purchase of the route into St. Louis in 1936, a garage was opened at Baxter Springs, Kan., which soon became an important fueling point. The gasoline tax at that time was $3\frac{1}{2}$ cents per gallon in Missouri, 3 cents in Oklahoma, and 2 cents in Kansas. Therefore, Harrell decided that all gasoline used in that area would be pumped at Baxter Springs, which was only seven miles west of the Missouri line and even closer to the Oklahoma line. In addition, Baxter Springs is approximately midway between St. Louis and Dallas. In 1940, an additional maintenance facility was added at St. Louis to handle the eastern area of the system, specifically, the newly acquired Illinois and Indiana routes of Yellow Transit.

In effect, the Yellow Transit system was comprised of operating units, reasonably autonomous, but with strong central control from Oklahoma City. The operation functioned smoothly, at least in part because of good employee relations. The pay scale was higher than that prevailing in the industry. The first Teamsters' Union contract involving Yellow Transit drivers concerned only recognition of the union since Yellow Transit was at the time paying above union scale. Harrell and Nash realized that Yellow Transit would become a prime union target, and they took the initiative in the original negotiations in the belief that it would give them a more advantageous bargaining position. In addition, the company offered such benefits as group life and accident insurance for employees. Yellow Transit had such a program long before other companies in the industry; by the time labor contracts contained such provisions, the Yellow Transit insurance plans were well established. The company also granted vacations to its personnel before the practice was generally adopted in the trucking industry.

Harrell's policy was to employ men for all positions, including the secretaries, stenographers, and clerks (the shortage of men during World War II ended this practice). Moreover, the Harrell policy favored men with families to support; they were regarded as more stable.

Yellow Transit was also known for its policies regarding equipment. Harrell believed that trucks, trailers, tractors, and all other equipment should reflect the personality of the company; as a result, Yellow Transit vehicles were clean and well maintained. Each tractor was assigned to a driver who was personally responsible for its appearance, repair, and use. Each man followed a preventive maintenance schedule and reported any unusual problem. Such a program was undoubtedly a wise one; the repair and maintenance of existing equipment cost less than frequent replacement of the running fleet, and each driver took a genuine interest in "his" tractor.

Yellow Transit bought only Fruehauf trailers for the tractors during Harrell's time, partly because of a long friendship with Harvey and Roy Fruehauf. Harrell kept the trailer fleet as new as was practical and made it a rule to trade in the old trailers of companies added to the system. During the late 1930's, when Yellow Transit was expanding rapidly, the company was able to keep its trailer fleet modern through trade-ins.

Yellow Transit was concerned early about weight distribution in the trailers and its relation to damage, shifting, and loading. Naturally, the company was anxious to maximize the use of space while minimizing damage. Ideas concerning weight distribution were checked out by varying the loads in the trailers and then weighing the rig. As a result of its experiments in this area, the company won the appreciation of highway commissioners and officials.

At one point, Yellow Transit installed translucent panels or squares in the roofs of the trailers so that stackers and unloaders would be able to see the labels on the cargo inside. Fragile items and boxes bound for the same destinations could be more readily sorted out. The result was a reduction in overages, shortages, and damages, known in the trade as OS&D.

For a truckline, the problem of tires is particularly significant because of the large investment involved; adding a few miles to the life of each tire in a fleet can make a great cost difference. Orginally, cotton cord tires were standard equipment, and these tended to expand in the hot summers of Texas, Oklahoma, Kansas, and Missouri. Two tires side by side on a rear axle would actually swell until they rubbed together, creating a fire hazard and causing rapid wear. Eventually, the Goodrich Rubber Company marketed a rayon cord tire that was vastly superior, but this was manufactured only in sizes suitable for Yellow Transit's smaller equipment. For larger equipment requiring twelve-cord tires, this type of tire was not available.

During this period, the Firestone Tire and Rubber Company was in the practice of sending unmarked tires to Yellow Transit; Harrell maintained that the rubber company's proving ground for truck tires was Yellow Transit routes. The lack of suitable tires for the large equipment bothered Harrell so much that he cornered Bob Hill, the Firestone engineer for the Amarillo branch, and asked why Firestone did not manufacture a twelve-ply rayon tire. Hill took the suggestion to Firestone headquarters at Akron, Ohio. The engineers and designers there were skeptical, but Harvey Firestone, Jr. became interested and flew to Oklahoma City for a discussion of the problem with Harrell. As a result, Firestone produced a twelve-ply tire, and Yellow Transit purchased the entire first production run at $48 per tire. At the time, eight-ply tires were costing the company $68 each. The new tires—the first modern heavy-duty tires—were a great success. Some years later, Harrell was quoted as saying, "It made Firestone a million."

The handling of employee relations and the solving of the tire problem are examples of Yellow Transit initiative. Such farsighted activities were an integral part of the operation. Both Harrell and Nash were convinced that, where problems demanded solution, the sensible thing was to plunge in and at least help mold the outcome.

Another result of this philosophy was the establishment of the Southwest Motor Freight Bureau at Dallas. The Motor Carrier Act of 1935 required the publication of and adherence to rates and fares, and the Dallas bureau functioned as the tariff-publishing agent for the carriers of the region. The Yellow Transit man involved in the establishment of the bureau was Nash, who also played an influential role in creating the Middlewest Motor Freight Bureau at Kansas City.

3 / FURTHER EXPANSION AND PROFITS

The May 10, 1937 agreement, which divided the partnership interests of the Harrell brothers, left A. J. Harrell in complete control of the Yellow Transit Company. This change in ownership was approved by the Interstate Commerce Commission on March 7, 1939. The major policy difference between the two had concerned expansion of Yellow Transit, and so, once freed of his brother's constraining influence, the new owner moved quickly to expand the system. Even before ICC approval, Yellow Transit had submitted the plans for purchase, control, and merger of Bryan Motor Freight Lines and the Yellow Cab Transit Company of Missouri, and for mergers with the Enders line into San Antonio and with Kern Motor Express of Illinois and Indiana. Each of these proposals was approved in time; Yellow Transit lines were being expanded rapidly.

On Dec. 8, 1939, Yellow Transit applied to the ICC for approval to purchase the properties of Frank L. Holsapple of Vincennes, Ind. The Holsapple Truck Lines operated about 380 miles of route between St. Louis and Evansville, between Lawrenceville and Robinson, Ill., and between Vincennes and Louisville via Washington, Paoli, and Greenville, Ind.

The St. Louis-Evansville portion exactly paralleled existing Yellow Transit routes, but it was the Louisville entry that made this purchase desirable. The agreed-upon price was $15,171 cash, which included the transfer of sixteen vehicles from Holsapple to Yellow Transit. In deciding favorably on Dec. 16, 1940, the ICC stated that:

Consummation of the purchase would permit numerous economies to be realized through elimination of duplicate administrative and operating func-

tions; and necessity for interchange and expenses and delays incident thereto
would be eliminated. . . . It was testified that a savings of from eight to ten
hours in transit time can be effected on shipments moving from Louisville via
St. Louis to southwestern points.[1]

The subsequent appearance of Yellow Transit Company vehicles in
Louisville produced an unexpected result: on May 16, 1941, the Louisville Taxicab and Transfer Company filed action against Yellow Transit. The issue concerned the use of the trademark "Yellow"; the taxicab
company maintained that it had operated in Louisville first and that an
undue nuisance was created by another company's use of the name. On
Dec. 23, 1943, the District Court for the Western District of Kentucky,
Louisville Division, held that the taxicab company was justified in pre-
venting the Yellow Transit Company from using the word "Yellow" in
connection with its operations and advertising in Louisville and Jeffer-
son County, Ky.[2] Harrell appealed, and, on Feb. 8, 1945, the Circuit
Court of Appeals for the Sixth District overruled the district court and
held as follows: "Appellant should be permitted the continued use of its
yellow painted trucks unchanged, in the movement of goods while engaged in interstate freight transportation in and out of Louisville,
Kentucky."[3]

On Dec. 3, 1940, Yellow Transit was again before the ICC with a plan
for expansion; the objective was Chicago. The company proposed to
purchase the operating rights of the Mid-Continent Freight Lines, Incorporated, of Mattoon, Ill., for $20,000. Mid-Continent had been in-
corporated originally as the Chester Miller Transfer Company, but, on
July 25, 1939, became Mid-Continent Freight Lines. The routes
authorized blanketed central Illinois, specifically between Mattoon and
Chrisman, Danville, Robinson, Lawrenceville, Centralia, Vandalia,
Hillsboro, Bloomington, and Peoria. In addition, Mid-Continent operated from Mattoon to St. Louis. On May 23, 1940, Mid-Continent had
received ICC approval for a route into Chicago via Champaign. The
total route mileage amounted to 1,200 miles.

Twenty days after the petition was filed, the commission acted in
favor of Yellow Transit, pointing out that the proposed combination

[1]Interstate Commerce Commission. "Yellow Cab Transit Company (Oklahoma)
—Purchase—Frank L. Holsapple," *Reports, Motor Carrier Cases*, XXXV (Washington: U.S. Gov't Printing Office), pp. 208-10.
[2]*Louisville Taxicab and Transfer Company* v. *Yellow Cab Transit Company*
(1943), 53 Fed. Supp., 272.
[3]147 Fed. Rept., 2d ser., 407.

would eliminate St. Louis interchange and would save ten to twelve hours on shipments from central Illinois to the southwest. A final comment by the commission was, "Other motor carriers render competitive service throughout the considered territory."[4] This was the first time that the preservation of competition had been mentioned in any of the Yellow Transit expansion cases.

Apparently, the competition became too severe, for on March 22, 1941 Yellow Transit Company sought authority to acquire part of the operating rights of the Ethington Freight Lines, owned by Ernest E. Ethington, which also had its headquarters at Mattoon. Yellow Transit sought two routes from St. Louis to Chicago. The first was through Litchfield, Mattoon, and Kankakee; the second followed U.S. Highway 40 from St. Louis to Effingham, and then to Chicago via Mattoon, Paris, and Danville. On July 3, 1941, the ICC granted permission.[5] The Ethington Freight Lines also held operating rights for livestock from Mattoon to Indianapolis; broomcorn from Neoga, Ill. and points in Coles County to St. Louis, Milwaukee, and Wausau, Wis.; and malt beverages from Milwaukee and St. Louis to Mattoon, with empty-container hauling privileges in the opposite direction. These rights were retained by the Ethington company, which continued to operate on a smaller scale.

The final expansion undertaken by Harrell concerned operating rights on two portions of a route from Kansas City-Illinois Motor Express, Incorporated. The plan was submitted to the ICC on April 20, 1942, and was approved on May 7. The price of $5,750 covered rights for operation between Boonville, Mo. and Kansas City, Kan., via U.S. Highway 40, and between Boonville and National Stock Yards, Ill., via the same highway. In effect, the purchase permitted Yellow Transit to operate between Kansas City and St. Louis by direct route. The savings for the company, which had formerly hauled St. Louis-Kansas City freight via Springfield, was 214 miles or approximately ten hours. Just two intermediate points could be served—Boonville and Rocheport, just off U.S. Highway 40 on the Missouri River.[6]

[4]Interstate Commerce Commission, "Yellow Cab Transit Co.—Purchase—Mid-Continent Freight Lines, Inc.," *Reports, Motor Carrier Cases*, XXXVI (Washington: U.S. Gov't Printing Office), p. 239.

[5]Interstate Commerce Commission, "Yellow Cab Transit Co.—Purchase—Ernest E. Ethington," *Reports, Motor Carrier Cases*, XXXVII (Washington: U.S. Gov't Printing Office), pp. 20-21.

[6]Interstate Commerce Commission, "Yellow Cab Transit Co.—Purchase—Kansas City-Illinois Express, Inc.," *Reports, Motor Carriers*, XXXVIII (Washington: U.S. Gov't Printing Office), p. 284.

The addition of one truckline occurred in quite a different manner. Carl Powers, the agent for Yellow Transit at Guthrie, Okla., also owned an intrastate truckline from Guthrie through Edmond to Oklahoma City. He wished to sell the line, but only to Yellow Transit. Unfortunately, Yellow Transit neither wanted nor needed the additional operating authority since the company already had a route for the twenty miles from Oklahoma City to Guthrie. Finally, in desperation, Evans A. Nash offered one dollar, and, to his astonishment, Powers accepted.

The result of Harrell's expansion policy was a far-flung truckline operating primarily in a north-south direction from Chicago, Louisville, and Evansville to San Antonio, Houston, and Amarillo. His company, which had grown out of a taxicab operation at Oklahoma City, had become an established business in its own right.[7]

Success of the growing company depended upon its ability to absorb the additions, a problem made more difficult by the Great Depression. Certainly, one of the key factors in the stability of Yellow Transit during this period was service; the company set fast schedules and adhered to them. The equipment maintenance program and the search for improved tires, for example, were undertaken in large measure to avoid breakdowns on the road and delays in delivery. Furthermore, the company tried to avoid making delivery promises that it could not keep; as a result, shippers felt they could rely on Yellow Transit.

The service feature also included efforts to produce a smoother operation through careful scheduling. Arrivals and departures were spaced to avoid jamming; the flow of merchandise over the docks was controlled, and every effort was made to reap the most efficient production from equipment, people, and physical facilities. The entire operation was designed to handle less-than-truckload freight exclusively from the north to the southwest. For hauls in the opposite direction, Yellow Transit also was eager to handle truckload traffic because the volume of available business was much less. The largest percentage of the traffic was southbound.

Communication problems can develop in a transportation company that operates over a large area. Decreased employee contact, for ex-

---

[7]Although Yellow Cab Transit Company was the official name, the company had done business for several years under the label of Yellow Transit Company. On Dec. 12, 1942, the name was officially changed. Corporate minutes of Yellow Transit Co., Dec. 12, 1942.

ample, tends to destroy the atmosphere of cooperation, which can sometimes make the difference between a workable arrangement and failure. The seniority system of advancement was adopted, therefore, and no one was forgotten in an outpost. Lack of ready interchange can also snarl operations and prevent the tracing of shipments. Yellow Transit Company was one of the first trucking companies to establish a teletype system for transmitting information over the trucking routes. The Kansas City terminal could inform the Oklahoma City terminal, for example, that three trucks had been dispatched to them, and, moreover, that the departure times had been 1:00, 3:00, and 4:00 P.M. In this way, the Oklahoma City dock could be prepared for arrivals and any unusual event could be reported. As one of the few companies with a system of fast and reliable communication between offices and terminals, Yellow Transit enjoyed a superior operational position and competitive advantage.

Yellow Transit could offer such special services only because the freight hauled tended to be of the high quality, "able-to-pay" variety. The company tried to appeal to the market for carrying packaged manufactured goods that required speed of delivery plus reasonable guarantee that the items would arrive when promised. Naturally, the rates charged for this type of service were somewhat higher on the average than the rates assessed on traffic in general; in fact, Yellow Transit was known as a high-rate carrier.

NASH'S CONTRIBUTION

As financial manager, Evans A. Nash handled the work concerned with the ICC, such as annual reports, materials for hearings, petitions for expansion, change of service, and so forth. The success of each major proposal submitted during this era to the ICC by Yellow Transit is testimony to Nash's skill. He was also the day-to-day manager of the company. Harrell was often absent because of his many other business interests, and he openly stated that Nash was hired partially as a "balance wheel" to keep the company running on a regular basis.

In 1931, before Nash was associated directly with the Yellow Transit Company, he was concerned with methods of measuring the profitability of the truckline. As accountant for the company, he devised some standard comparisons. For example, a nine-month report for January through September, 1931 contained the following:

During the nine months the company has operated 352,515 Tractor Miles. The average revenue, per tractor mile, was 39 cents, leaving a net profit of nine cents per tractor mile.

Forwarded freight for the first nine months, from your principal stations, was as follows:

Oklahoma City	6,124,379 pounds
Dallas	5,815,453 pounds
Kansas City	4,013,392 pounds
Tulsa	3,668,264 pounds
Total	19,621,488 pounds

Revenue per ton of handled freight amounted to approximately $98.11. Operating expense totaled $81.28, leaving a net profit of $16.83 per ton.[8]

Within a month after joining Yellow Transit as vice-president in early 1933, Nash attended a trucking industry meeting at Kansas City of operators from several midwestern and plains states. The new Yellow Transit man tried to learn as much as he could from the people in the industry, but virtually no trucker was able to answer Nash's questions concerning revenue per mile, revenue per hundredweight, or average revenue per day. Upon returning to Oklahoma City, he set about the task of developing some meaningful financial standards for control purposes.

The careful accounting system that Yellow Transit developed involved extensive regular reports. Each month the following charts and tables were prepared: Balance Sheet; Statement of Profit and Loss; Miscellaneous Line accounts (such as drivers' salaries, tractor depreciation, truck depreciation, tire repairs, and toll bridge fees); Gasoline and Lubricants; Shop Expense; Station Expenses; Maintenance and Repair; Licenses and Taxes; Administrative Expense; Statistics, Tonnage, and Cost; Analysis of Unpaid C.O.D.'s; Analysis of Balance All Stations; and Analysis of Balance Due the Company. Considerable detail was required in each account, and, by comparing the monthly statements, the managers of the company were able to single out areas of high cost and weakness, and also areas of outstanding performance.

Perhaps one of the most interesting original charts was Statistics, Tonnage, and Cost. Each month was compared with the corresponding

[8]Evans A. Nash and Co., Accountants and Auditors, "Reports of Operations, Yellow Cab Transit Company," Sept. 30, 1931.

month from the previous year, and, in addition, it was easily checked against the previous months of the same year. Below is an example of the November, 1933 chart:

Station	Freight Forwarded	Freight Received	Total	Cost
Kansas City	1,023,992	215,914	1,239,906	$0.120
Tulsa	486,535	483,468	952,003	0.107
Oklahoma City	492,912	1,285,839	1,778,751	0.080
Dallas	473,175	359,598	832,773	0.141
Fort Worth	68,820	157,197	226,017	0.160
Houston	522,514	189,669	712,183	0.103
Miscellaneous	48,266	406,529	454,795	0.120
Totals	3,098,214	3,092,214	6,196,428	

This chart is interesting from several standpoints. First, the amount of freight forwarded from Kansas City and received at Oklahoma City shows that Yellow Transit Company tonnage flowed toward the south. Second, the fact that the flow of traffic between Houston and Dallas was balanced is also confirmed. Third, the balance between forwarded and received freight for the system as a whole might indicate a fairly closed operation, with most of the tonnage originating and being delivered by Yellow Transit itself.

The particular schedules and charts included in the monthly analysis were changed and presumably updated from time to time. Strangely enough, one of the first deletions was the Statistics, Tonnage, and Cost report. By November, 1940, the list of monthly reports had been further modified to include a Transportation account, which replaced Miscellaneous Line accounts and Shop Expense; a separate category for Traffic or Sales Expense; and the combination of the old balance reports into an Accounts Receivable section. During the first decade of its existence, the Yellow Transit Company's system of financial controls was sophisticated in comparison to that of most companies then in the motor carrier industry.

COMPANY FINANCES

As Yellow Transit became a profitable unit in the Harrell brothers' partnership, the policy was to retain the majority of the earnings in the business. The funds were used to modernize facilities, replace inadequate terminals, purchase new equipment, and expand the system. In 1934, a cash dividend was declared; by 1936, the brothers had begun to retain all earnings. The company had 250 shares outstanding from 1924 to December, 1936, with a par value of $100 each. At the end of 1936, however, a 9 to 1 stock dividend was declared, and the capital stock account of the company increased from $25,000 to $250,000. By January, 1940, the capital account had risen to $350,000, again through the declaration of stock dividends; by January, 1941, the capital stock figure was recorded at $500,000, still with a par value of $100. This growth was particularly impressive, considering the fact that no outside capital had been added during the period. The net worth of the company had increased from $104,158 in 1931 to $1,311,090 at the close of 1943.

Profits, of course, had to be substantial to allow for such growth. Table 1 summarizes the record of the company by selected years during the periods of ownership by the brothers and then by A. J. Harrell alone. The return on net worth figures for the company was nothing short of fantastic: during the most intense and long-lived business downturn in the nation's history, Yellow Transit earned 33 per cent on investment in 1934. The 1937 figure of 13.5 per cent, while also impressive, reflected the internal strife that was plaguing the company.

One factor behind the increase in gross revenue was the expansion of the system through the purchase of going concerns. However, the total gross revenue for the enlarged Yellow Transit Company was greater than the sum for the separate companies before merging. The market share of Yellow Transit increased, both through a more intensive coverage of existing service areas and through the creation of a longer-haul service to newly added territories of the system. Primarily through the efforts of A. J. Harrell, the Oklahoma City-Tulsa run of the Yellow Transit Company of 1929 had evolved into a major truckline with annual revenues approaching $3 million.

Total assets grew as the company expanded, with the largest part in

TABLE 1
Company Growth by Selected Years, 1931-43

Year	Total Revenue	Net Income	Income as a Per Cent of Revenue	Total Assets	Income as a Per Cent of Assets	Net Worth	Income as a Per Cent of Net Worth
1931	$ 231,472	$ 32,290	13.9	$ 131,583	24.4	$ 104,158	31.0
1934	355,654	42,973	12.0	160,862	26.7	130,175	33.0
1937	837,323	39,651	4.7	565,176	7.0	290,815	13.6
1941	2,154,750	195,907	9.0	1,218,092	16.0	975,092	20.0
1943	2,705,729	170,899	6.3	1,822,010	9.3	1,311,090	13.0

SOURCE: Figures for 1931, 1934, 1937, and 1941 are from company records; 1943 figures are from Yellow Transit's annual report to the Interstate Commerce Commission.

the investment in operating property. In 1931, the figure for operating properties, less depreciation, was $106,360. Equipment, terminal, and similar investments had grown to $434,730 by 1937, and to $933,762 by 1941.

Some investment in nonoperating property had been made through the years, but the figure was small. At the close of 1943, the nonoperating property list, totaling $195,459, was as follows: St. Louis—land, $37,271, and buildings, $20,000; Dallas—land, $79,605, and buildings, $36,396; Ardmore, Okla.—land, $1,169; San Antonio—land, $15,289; and Springfield, Mo.—land, $5,729. In addition, the company had investments of $58,668 in filling stations, held 100 shares in the Victory Cartage Company, and owned one share of the stock of the Spring Valley Butter Company.

On Oct. 24, 1942, a shipment tendered by the M. G. Gintz Company of East St. Louis brought Yellow Transit before the Supreme Court of the United States. The shipment, consigned to the F.A.S. Officers' Club mess at the Fort Sill military reservation in Oklahoma, contained 225 cases of wine and liquor—but, in 1942, Oklahoma was dry. On Oct. 26, the truck carrying the cases rolled into the Yellow Transit terminal at Oklahoma City; there, the whiskey was seized by a party of men headed by Walter B. Johnson, Commissioner of Public Safety of the State of Oklahoma. On Dec. 24, 1942, in the District Court for the Western District of Oklahoma, the Yellow Transit Company won a court order for the return of the shipment for delivery to its original destination. Moreover, on July 26, 1943, the Circuit Court of Appeals for the Tenth Circuit affirmed the district court judgment.

However, the commissioner was unyielding, and on Jan. 6 and 7, 1944, the case was argued before the Supreme Court. In its decision of March 13, 1944, the Supreme Court held as follows: "No Oklahoma law purports on its face to prohibit or regulate interstate shipments of liquor into and through the state to another state, or to an area subject to the exclusive jurisdiction of the United States."[9]

The court affirmed the right of the Yellow Transit Company to haul items in interstate commerce through Oklahoma since no Oklahoma law was broken. Had the shipment been bound for a point other than government property, the outcome surely would have been different; as it was, Justices Frankfurter and Roberts dissented.

The year of 1943 was the last full year in which A. J. Harrell owned

[9] *Johnson et al.* v. *Yellow Cab Transit Co.* (1944), 321 U.S. 383.

the Yellow Transit Company. According to the annual report, the average work force that year amounted to 562 people with an average yearly compensation of $2,114 and a total payroll of $1,188,362. Drivers made up 129 of the employees; their average pay was $2,654. In the supervisory and official category, Yellow Transit employed eight, with an average yearly salary of $10,075. The 562 people had driven, maintained, or managed 142 vehicles; these vehicles had been driven 9,296,-138 miles in intercity service and had consumed 1,937,659 gallons of gasoline and 90,212 quarts of oil. Yellow Transit was already a long-haul carrier; the average haul that year was 468.9 miles.

The record was impressive in every respect, but Harrell had decided to sell his most valuable business asset, the Yellow Transit Company. He had entered his sixties, and was feeling less and less able to manage his many interests; among them, the truckline was the most demanding. It had become even more of a problem as World War II began. Oil and gasoline were in short supply; replacement equipment was not available; and maintenance crews had to work overtime and display unusual skill and inventiveness in order to keep the trucks rolling. Frequently, tires were removed from incoming trucks or trailers and put on outgoing vehicles. To add to the difficulty, service demands became more and more urgent; vital war materials had to be moved in the shortest time possible with the least expenditure of resources. Harrell was bothered most, perhaps, by the drafting of his employees. As is often the case in one-man operations, he had developed a paternalistic attitude toward the Yellow Transit workers. In short, Harrell was ready to sell his truckline if he could find the proper buyer.

When a New York broker, A. W. Porter, approached Harrell with the idea of buying shares of company stock, Harrell promptly informed him that stock was not for sale but that the entire truckline was. A deal was worked out, but Harrell included a sixty-day time limit. Nothing was heard from Porter within the period, but shortly thereafter he reported that he was ready to close the deal. Harrell replied that the time limit was up, that Yellow Transit had netted some $42,000 in the sixty days, and that the selling price had now increased by that amount. A few days later, Porter arrived in Oklahoma City, cash in hand, and purchased the capital stock of the Yellow Transit Company. The security holders' list at the close of 1943 had read: A. J. Harrell, 4,649 shares; Evans A. Nash, 150 shares; and W. L. Stevenson, 1 share. At the end of 1944, the list had been altered to read: Evans A. Nash, 1 share; A. W. Porter, 4,998 shares; and R. C. Hardy, 1 share. The first period in the history of the Yellow Transit Freight Lines was over.

4 / PROGRESS—THEN POVERTY

The second period of Yellow Transit Company history began on Nov. 27, 1944 when 4,998 of the 5,000 authorized shares were transferred to the new owner, Arlington W. Porter of Port Washington, N.Y. Evans A. Nash and Robert C. Hardy, who held the remaining two shares as qualifying shares, joined Porter as the directors of Yellow Transit.[1] Each was an officer of the company: Nash, president and treasurer; Porter, vice-president; and Hardy, secretary. A few employees devoted to Harrell left the company, but, in general, Yellow Transit personnel changed little.

Nash, formerly the company's vice-president, had been the operating officer under Harrell and was thoroughly familiar with policies and procedures; in fact, he had been instrumental in developing the methods of operation. His success in keeping the trucks rolling during World War II led to his appointment to the Advisory Committee of the Office of Defense Transportation. In addition, Nash served as a director of and chairman of the Transportation Committee of the U.S. Chamber of Commerce and was a member of the advisory committee of the Office of Price Administration and of the War Labor Board.

---

[1]At this time, Yellow Transit was one of 1,337 Class I Intercity Motor Carriers of property according to the U.S. Bureau of the Census, *Statistical Abstract of the United States: 1951* (71st ed.; Washington: U.S. Gov't Printing Office, 1951), p. 515.

Many of the meetings of these committees and boards were held in Washington, D.C., and Nash became a frequent visitor in the East. He often conferred in New York City with Porter, who, in turn, made several trips to the home office at Oklahoma City and toured the system with Nash.

Naturally, some differences in Yellow Transit operations resulted from the new ownership. On March 10, 1945, a Delaware Corporation, Yellow Terminals, Inc., was formed. Five days later, on March 15, 1945, the Yellow Equipment Company was formed under the laws of the state of Illinois. These two companies were wholly owned subsidiaries of the Yellow Transit Company and, as their names imply, were involved in equipment and terminal operations. The new arrangement allowed the subsidiaries to make equipment purchases and build terminals that, in turn, were leased to the parent company. Yellow Transit could possibly save on its tax bill by taking advantage of certain tax rules that permitted lease payments to subsidiaries as legitimate expense items; to the subsidiaries, such payments were gross revenues from which operating expenses were deducted before taxes were paid.

The company's tax payments could be thereby reduced, but the cost of operating three companies—as opposed to operating one consolidated company—may not have been advantageous. Apparently, the new owners of Yellow Transit were satisfied, but Nash expressed subtle disapproval in his annual report for 1945 to Porter, chairman of the board of directors. A letter of transmittal and explanation of Feb. 28, 1946 read, in part, as follows:

> In the year 1945, the Yellow Transit Co. (parent company) had an operating income of $2,817,895.33, an increase of $151,973.46 over that realized in 1944.
>
> Prior to provision for income tax and payment of rents to subsidiaries, the company realized a net income of $305,843.51 or $18,192.28 in excess of that for 1944. The Operating Ratio, prior to subsidiary rents and income tax, in 1945 was 89.15%, as contrasted with 89.12% for 1944.
>
> After making provision for income taxes in the sum of $21,649.32 and payment of $257,033.37 in rents to Yellow Terminals, Inc., and Yellow Equipment Co., the net transferred to surplus account was $27,160.82.

This mild comment was the first expression of what was to become a major policy difference between Nash and the new ownership. The balance sheets for the Yellow Transit Company, Yellow Terminals, Inc., and Yellow Equipment Company, as contained in the annual report for 1945, disclosed another point of departure. The balance sheet for However, Nash was concerned that still higher motor carrier rates would the parent company indicated investments in Yellow Terminals of $646,880 and in Yellow Equipment of $270,802. These transactions were consummated during the first year of the subsidiaries' existence. The balance sheet for Yellow Terminals duly recorded capital stock and paid-in surplus of $646,880, but, in addition, it reported "Surplus—From Appreciation of Assets" of $420,760. The Yellow Equipment capital stock and surplus account contained an item of $416,366 from appreciation of assets, making the total appreciated surplus for the consolidated companies $837,126. To a conservative accountant like Nash, such a reevaluation of assets by appraisal was questionable at best.

Another problem arose on April 19, 1945, when the Yellow Equipment Company obtained cash on a mortgage in the amount of $375,000. On the same day, the company paid the same amount to Porter, who liquidated his indebtedness on July 5, 1945 by selling 1,250 shares of Yellow Transit Company stock to Yellow Equipment. No change in control resulted from this transaction, since the equipment company was a wholly owned subsidiary of Yellow Transit, still completely controlled by Porter. Such maneuvers were totally objectionable to Nash.

Nash took over complete operation of the Yellow Transit Company during the closing months of World War II. In 1945 and 1946, the principal difficulty was the lack of parts and equipment (a problem throughout the trucking industry), but by 1948, when the shortages had been eased, Yellow Transit had a new problem—a lack of funds for needed improvements and replacements. The difficulty was compounded by postwar price inflation as released demand, coupled with scarce supply, resulted in rising prices and costs. The transportation industry and other industries with price controls helped check the rise somewhat because of the "regulatory lag" in approving proposed price or rate increases. The delay on the part of state and national regulatory commissions in granting such increases sometimes leads to a profit squeeze, and Yellow Transit found itself in just such a predicament at the end of the war. For example, from 1944 to 1945, operating revenues increased $151,973, but expenses increased $146,373 during the same period, according to a Feb. 28, 1946 letter of transmittal in the companies' annual report for 1945. Management attributed most of the expense increase to rising price levels.

Nash was also concerned with the relationship of motor carrier rates to the rates charged by competitive modes of transportation, especially the railroads. Motor carrier rates were, in general, already higher than rail rates; the difference in the services offered and in the varying requirements of shippers provided the motor carriers with their market.

However, Nash was concerned that still higher motor carrier rates would cause substantial diversion of traffic from the highways to the railroads. In his February letter of transmittal, he reported that "the motor freight industry is faced with a serious problem of securing compensatory rates for its traffic."

The first portion of Nash's short reign as president of Yellow Transit was successful despite the basic changes in the corporate structure of the company and its ownership. Porter was an investor, not a truckline man, and was apparently unfamiliar with company management in general. Consequently, he relied on a group of associates, some of whom were lawyers specializing in taxation, corporate existence, and so forth, for advice on the corporate structure of Yellow Transit, financing arrangements, investment decisions involving major expenditures, and, in general, policy decisions at the highest level. Because of his long experience in the motor carrier business, Nash was consulted constantly at first by Porter and his cohorts. As the group gained confidence in its own abilities, however, Nash was less and less the policy maker and company planner. Nevertheless, the balance of power remained with Nash while Porter lived, but after his death in September, 1948, major changes in direct management occurred.

EQUIPMENT AND COST PROBLEMS

One of the most critical problems facing the truckline during the first years of the Nash presidency was that of old equipment. Replacement of total units was out of the question until after the war—well into 1947 —and their cost was almost prohibitive. The companies' annual report for 1947 listed the model year of the 185 power units as follows: 1935, 5; 1936, 9; 1937, 14; 1938, 24; 1939, 5; 1940, 25; 1941, 32; 1944, 19; 1945, 20; 1946, 11; and 1947, 21. Thus, at the end of 1947, 114 tractors, or 61 per cent, were of prewar vintage. As a result, maintenance costs were high. In addition, experienced mechanics were scarce; consequently, even when good replacement parts were available, satisfactory garage work could not be assured. Total maintenance costs from 1944 to 1947 rose substantially, as shown by the following figures from the companies' 1947 annual report: 1947, $568,442; 1946, $482,447; 1945, $424,303; and 1944, $324,632. Included in the costs for 1946 and 1947 was the rebuilding of 227 motors in the Oklahoma City shops.

The purchase of any equipment that became available had short-run appeal, but, as indicated in an information letter of October, 1948, entitled "Yellow Transit Co., and Subsidiaries," Yellow Transit kept the long run in view. Only gasoline-fueled White and Mack truck-tractors, considered suitable for the topography of the area covered, were put on the road during the immediate postwar period. Standardization of the parts inventory, mechanics' familiarity with repair, and overhead problems were the reasons for this policy. Over a period of years, it seems likely that standardization did indeed reduce costs.

The tire supply was also of great concern to the company during World War II and in the years immediately following. Despite an effort to conserve vehicles and fuel, tires still had to be replaced. Both tires and tubes were scarce and their quality was inferior. The synthetic tube, stamped with a red band or with S-4, was available but difficult to repair.

The year 1944 was the worst, and on inventory day, Dec. 31, Yellow Transit had on hand at its Oklahoma City garage 483 rims in need of tires. The severe shortage necessitated emergency procedures; tires were removed from incoming vehicles and put on equipment otherwise ready to roll out. As the tire and tube market eased following the war, extensive purchases had to be made to replace the depleted inventory, and in 1945, 1946, and 1947, a total of $314,397 was spent.

Nash was especially interested in the tire stock and was eager to improve the condition of the "company rubber." At the end of 1948, approximately 3,840 tires were branded Yellow Transit. The letter of transmittal for the annual report for 1948 contained the following: "A recent survey of the tire conditions at the principal garages indicated a very favorable position. In fact, the company in comparison with companies of a similar size in 15 other states showed that our tire condition was second-best." Although this statement fails to disclose the number of companies included in the comparison, at least Nash was satisfied that the Yellow Transit tire supply was in top condition.

Construction, halted during the war, began again in 1947; the Yellow Terminals subsidiary built three new terminals. The first to be completed was a 42-door unit on Harry Hines Blvd. in Dallas, a major breaking-and-gathering point; garage facilities for repair and maintenance of the fleet for the southern region of the system were also constructed. The old Dallas terminal had been too small and had created a bottleneck in the over-all operation of the company. A similar situation existed at St. Louis, the breaking-and-gathering point for the northern region of the Yellow Transit system. In 1947, a 42-door terminal was constructed on Chouteau Ave., and a new garage facility contract was let for a repair shop.

A 36-door terminal was purchased in Chicago in 1947, and after some rehabilitation, was occupied January, 1948. At Ardmore, Okla., a highway project necessitated the construction of a new terminal with 12 doors, which was opened in 1947. Finally, in February, 1948, work began on a new terminal at San Antonio.

Other terminal expenses rose rapidly during the postwar years. The rise in the wages of dock workers was the biggest item of increase, although the new up-to-date facilities relieved the problem somewhat by substituting capital for labor. Nevertheless, from 1945 to 1946 alone, the labor bill for dock personnel jumped $72,566. Yellow Transit made every effort to increase efficiency at the dock and succeeded in cutting overtime and increasing the freight handled per man-hour. This, of course, helped offset the higher wage-per-hour outlay.

The pay for over-the-road drivers was also mounting steadily; labor contracts negotiated at the close of the war called for substantial increases. The annual report for 1947 states that the Yellow Transit dollar outlay for drivers was 29.1 per cent higher in 1947 than in 1946; the absolute increase was $102,645, for a 1947 total of $495,861. However, at the same time, new highway construction and improvements reduced the road-time between terminals.

Nash's first response to increasing costs in virtually every department was to encourage productivity increases wherever and whenever practicable. This plan involved a continual push for upgrading the traffic carried. The first phase was a campaign for "single-line" business— traffic that both originates and terminates on line—with the idea of capturing the total revenue for Yellow Transit. Generally speaking, when two or more carriers participate in a movement, the division of the revenues is not strictly on a mileage basis. Thus, if one carrier trucks an item for 400 miles and another carrier hauls the final 100 miles, the division of revenues would tend to be something like 75-25 rather than 80-20. Single-line traffic was sought particularly in cases where Yellow Transit was authorized to make the complete haul. Perhaps the best example was traffic from Chicago to Dallas, which formerly had been routed by some other carrier to St. Louis and by Yellow Transit to Dallas. A great effort was made to pick up such traffic at Chicago.

Sometimes such "invading" upset competitors, but Yellow Transit offered superior service and was able to capture new traffic. Also, a survey of traffic flows often indicated specific moves that could be traded. In one case, a Chicago shipper tendered traffic to Yellow Transit at Chicago bound for St. Louis, but shipped Houston traffic by an alternate carrier from Chicago to St. Louis, where it was interchanged with Yellow Transit for Houston delivery. A Yellow Transit salesman was able to convince the shipper to switch the traffic on the Chicago-St. Louis portion and save transloading and interchange at St. Louis. Both carriers and the shipper benefited by this move.

A second part of the traffic improvement plan was an attempt to attract long-haul traffic. The annual report for 1948 gives the average lengths of haul for the period: 1948, 491 miles; 1947, 465 miles; 1946, 455 miles; 1945, 471 miles; and 1944, 482 miles.

The Yellow Transit policy of favoring less-than-truckload (L.T.L.) freight was continued through the 1944-48 period. The policy had been the idea of A. J. Harrell; he noted that, although handling costs for such traffic were higher than for full truckloads, rates were proportionately higher. In addition, Nash thought the market for such traffic was both firmer and more extensive. Fewer truckloads were offered Yellow Transit in 1947 than in 1946, and Nash cited this in the 1947 annual report as indication of the "gradual catching-up of production with demand." He further stated that, as a result, ". . . fill-in and drop shipments, in our opinion, should begin to climb, and it has been thought that attention now to the smaller shipments might have a material tendency to keep our volume up." Truckload (T.L.) traffic was also thought to be more vulnerable to railroad competition than the packaged-goods, L.T.L. market. Actually, Yellow Transit featured a preferred service, which appealed to shippers of small, high-rate goods.

CHANGES IN OPERATIONS

Shortly after the war, when scheduled operations were resumed, Yellow Transit adopted the following names for certain through-runs with the idea of using them in advertising: Dallas and St. Louis, "Longhorn"; Oklahoma City and St. Louis, "Plainsman"; Houston and St. Louis, "Exporter"; Kansas City and Oklahoma City, "K.C. Flyer"; Kansas City and Dallas, "Friendship"; and Wichita and Houston, "Jayhawker." These train-like names, however, were soon dropped; apparently, it was decided to advertise Yellow Transit, not the "Plainsman."

During the 1946-47 period, several purchases extended the Yellow Transit system. The most significant was the purchase of operating rights along U.S. Highway 40, from St. Louis to Indianapolis, from the

Brashear Freight Lines, Inc. Most of the U.S. 40 route in Illinois was already in the Yellow system, but the opening into the Indianapolis gateway established several new eastern connections.[2] The price of the new route was $8,500, which included no equipment, and the Interstate Commerce Commission approved the exchange on Sept. 23, 1946.

In the same year, Yellow Transit acquired operating rights over U.S. Highway 66 from Chicago to St. Louis. The objective here was not additional territory; U.S. 66 was the short route and saved twenty miles per trip. Hutchinson, Kan., was added to the company's operations in 1946. The purchase of operating rights along U.S. Highway 50 from the Esau Freight Lines was approved by the ICC on June 19, 1946.[3]

Finally, in the spring of 1947, Yellow Transit purchased the intrastate operating rights of the Long Motor Freight Lines for $12,500. The Long certificate did not extend the company system but, instead, opened to Yellow Transit several stations within the state of Oklahoma. The major stations added were Norman, Chickasha, Seminole, Lexington, and Purcell. The objective was intensive coverage of an area rather than addition of a route. Oklahoma City became a breaking point as a result of the purchase.

During the postwar period, Yellow Transit moved into new areas of supporting operations aimed at improving service for the shipping public. For example, a tracing section was organized on Aug. 1, 1946 to match lost-and-found freight and track down lost shipments. The new section reduced substantially the number of claims filed and paid and created goodwill among shippers by improving assurance of delivery.

The claims section of Yellow Transit apparently enjoyed an excellent reputation in the eyes of shippers, as indicated by the item included in the Feb. 17, 1947 letter of transmittal for the 1946 annual report:

> We find that in practically every instance where the Yellow Transit Co. may have participated in the haul, and a claim is filed, it is lodged with us. We then must trace and handle through all connections if the merchandise moved with an interchange. This creates a great burden on the Claim Department, but the claimant, under the law, has the privilege of filing with a participating carrier, and we seem to be the 'favored line'.

[2]Interstate Commerce Commission, "A. W. Porter—Control: Yellow Transit Company—Purchase (Portion)—Brashear Freight Lines, Inc.," *Reports, Motor Carrier Cases*, XLV (Washington: U.S. Gov't Printing Office), p. 811.

[3]Interstate Commerce Commission, "A. W. Porter—Control: Yellow Transit Co.—Purchase—A. M. Esau," *Reports, Motor Carrier Cases*, XL (Washington: U.S. Gov't Printing Office), p. 845.

Claims were cut further by the claim prevention section, created Jan. 1, 1947 to correct the conditions that produced claims in the first place. Basically, the plan was one of education; proper handling, stacking, and unloading of the merchandise and careful reading of labels and bills of lading were stressed.

One of the characteristics of the traffic flow of Yellow Transit had been the generally heavier movement of goods from the north to the south. This pattern continued through the postwar years and created a burden when an attempt was made to balance operations. In 1947, each of the following terminals had 25 per cent or more outbound loads than incoming loads: Louisville, 47 per cent; Chicago, 34; Oklahoma City, 28; St. Louis, 27; Indianapolis, 25; and Kansas City, 25. With the exception of Oklahoma City, these stations were all on the northern end of the system. At other stations, incoming loads exceeded outbound loads. The five most unbalanced locations were Ardmore, 53 per cent; Amarillo, 51; Springfield, 42; Wichita Falls, 31; and San Antonio, 16. These points were all in the southern part of the system.

The solution to the balance problem was not easily found; indeed, little progress was made during these years. The southbound traffic consisted mainly of high-rated manufactured goods in substantial volume; most of the flow to the north consisted of a lesser quantity of low-rated raw materials. Yellow Transit tended to avoid the low-rated traffic and, instead, endured the unbalanced traffic flow.

THE PROFIT PICTURE: 1948

Although the method of determining profitability was not indicated, Nash's annual report for 1948 to the board of directors ranked the ten most profitable stations for 1947 and 1948 as follows:

1948	1947
St. Louis	Kansas City
Chicago	St. Louis
Kansas City	Oklahoma City
Louisville	Houston
Indianapolis	Louisville
San Antonio	Wichita
Wichita	San Antonio
Oklahoma City	Fort Worth
Fort Worth	Indianapolis
Houston	Chicago

The 1948 report also showed increases in the amount of freight handled and in the number of miles it was hauled. The figures were as follows:

Years	Pounds	Miles
1944	273,604,183	8,416,500
1945	292,912,833	8,026,672
1946	321,899,116	8,606,133
1947	345,973,944	9,890,319
1948	395,103,962	12,143,263

The total revenue also increased as the company extended and intensified its operation. Table 2 compares the results of the 1945-48 period on a year-to-year basis. Although the figures are not outstanding, or indeed as high as those for Yellow Transit during the 1930's, the profit trend was generally upward. The revenue situation was especially healthy, because of the expanded system and the increase in rates effective in 1948. Yellow Transit estimated that its system average advanced approximately 15 per cent.

Behind the scenes, however, all was not in the best condition. Dealings between the parent company and its two subsidiaries had begun to disturb Nash more and more. The following passage, found in the annual report for 1947, clearly states his position:

Under the company's present lease requirements, for terminals and equipment, in my opinion, a problem is presented that may not be successfully handled. The lease requirements call for rentals aggregating $420,000.00 per year. This is an increase of $78,000.00 over that paid in 1947. Assuming the business has no slack in business, that it does not encounter any additional expense increases, that it runs on an even keel with the year just closed, then the rental requirements would amount to 86.4% of the net carrier operating income. Thus, it is readily noted, nothing of consequence is left to build up cash reserves or pay income taxes, and serious inroads will be made in equity capital. May I therefore call to the attention of the Board the suggestion made in my letter of July 3, 1947, reading in part as follows:
'It occurs to me that we should give some thoughts to a long-term financing program that will permit reduced amortization payments and thus permit the building up of cash reserves that may be used for necessary repairs or expansion. Money rates probably will increase rather than decrease in the future, and the time looks ripe for consideration of a broad, long-range program.'

Later Nash's position was supported by Ford K. Edwards of the ICC. In an Oct. 17, 1959 letter to Nash he wrote:

A recent examination of the accounts and records of your company and its wholly owned subsidiaries, Yellow Terminals, Inc., and Yellow Equipment Co., disclosed an apparent distortion of the Net Operating Revenue of Yellow

TABLE 2
Comparison of Total Revenues, 1945-48

Year	Total Revenue	Net Income	Income as a Per Cent of Revenue	Total Assets	Income as a Per Cent of Assets	Net Worth	Income as a Per Cent of Net Worth
1945	$2,841,124	$101,699	3.6	$3,186,609	3.2	$2,010,025	5.0
1946	3,279,166	227,467	6.8	3,076,119	7.4	1,961,220	11.6
1947	3,855,877	176,478	4.6	3,316,112	5.3	2,406,409	7.4
1948	5,132,393	282,584	5.5	3,508,356	8.0	1,919,218	14.6

SOURCE: Annual reports from president to chairman of the board, 1945-48.

Transit as a result of rental payments to the subsidiary companies being in excess of what it would have cost Transit had it retained ownership in the properties which were transferred to the subsidiaries in 1945.

Cash working capital has been depleted to a sometimes impossible low. This depletion has been caused by the use of operating capital to finance capital expenditures. The return to the operating company of its advances, viz: $287,774.68 as of December 31, 1947, will replenish its cash to the extent that creditable balances may be maintained in its various depository banks, and a nice saving in service charges will accrue.

Nash's suggestion was totally ignored by the group in control, however, and nothing was done to improve either the cash problem or the lease arrangements with the subsidiary companies. Apparently, Nash and the stockholders held differing views of the company. Nash concentrated on running a truckline, and the financial "dealings" were hampering effective operations; the owners presumably saw the truckline as only a part of the business. Moreover, they were apparently satisfied with their approach, for even more expansive plans of corporate structure were soon undertaken.

In the fall of 1948, Yellow Transit Systems, Inc. was organized under the laws of the state of Delaware. Yellow Transit Systems became the holder of the stock of the Yellow Transit Company. The Yellow family was now increased to four: the systems, the transit company, the equipment company, and the terminals. The effects of this maneuver were not immediately noticeable.

NASH-INVESTOR DISAGREEMENTS

In September, 1948, the death of Arlington W. Porter ended the working relationship between the old Yellow Transit Company of Evans Nash and the new investors. The termination was not immediate, but without Porter as chairman the new group moved further away from the counsel of Nash.

The decision concerning capital outlays is an example of the coming split. Nash listed several projects of prime importance in maintaining an efficient operation for Yellow Transit. Foremost was the need for additional space at Oklahoma City. The intensive coverage of Oklahoma points, especially following the purchase of intrastate rights from the Long Motor Freight Lines, brought large tonnages to the Oklahoma City terminal dock. For all its excellence, the old terminal—pride of A. J. Harrell—was too small to handle the volume. Dock space was crowding out adjacent repair facilities, and these, too, were bearing a heavier load.

The second floor of the terminal was crowded with general office personnel, even though the penthouse apartment on the third floor had been converted into office space. Storage facilities for records were so inadequate that most of the general data preserved at the behest of the ICC were moved to Dallas.

Nash recommended the construction of a new repair and maintenance facility incorporating changes for preventive maintenance work, for example, larger service racks for the bigger trucks. Separate housing for the repair facility would remove a fire hazard from the building that also housed a freight dock and the general offices. Another project that Nash considered urgent was the construction of a permanent loading apron at the Chicago terminal to relieve problems caused by improper drainage. He also recommended that small terminals be built at Austin and Wichita Falls, Tex.

Nash made several suggestions concerning the rolling stock, the other major area of capital outlay. For example, he recommended the purchase of thirty-six truck-tractors, five delivery trucks, and ten business coupes to replace equipment in use but unsafe on the roads. The purchase of additional vehicles was not proposed. The board of directors, however, did not follow his recommendations. Some substantial financial transactions were completed late in 1948, but they were far from those suggested by Nash.

The new group in power seemed to have grasped the significance of personal return, but they apparently failed to realize the necessity for a growing concern to retain earnings in order to finance expansion. In 1948, gross revenues of the truckline operation increased to $5,055,885, up 32 per cent from 1947; about half the increase could be attributed to the 15 per cent boost in rates effected in 1948.

Net income after taxes, figured on a comparable basis, jumped from $87,774 in 1947 to $169,392 in 1948. This 93 per cent increase assumed modest proportions in view of the dividend of $750,000 declared by the board of directors of the Yellow Transit Company. The intersubsidiary dealings that led to the dividend were particularly interesting. The earned surplus figure for the Yellow Transit Company, as of Jan. 1, 1948, was $377,796. Net income from operations added $169,392, and minor expense and tax adjustments added $71,077, for a normal year-end total of $618,266. Normal deductions from tax adjustments, transfer from earned to capital surplus accounts, and nonrecurring commission expenses totaled $260,798, which would have resulted in an earned surplus figure of $357,468 at year-end. However, some unusual additions and deductions left a quite different earned surplus figure.

The unusual additions were $200,000 in dividends from Yellow Terminals and $200,000 from the Yellow Equipment Company. In reality, Yellow Transit Company advanced $200,000 to each of the subsidiaries, and each subsidiary in turn declared a dividend of $200,000 to Yellow Transit. This maneuver brought the earned surplus figure up to $757,-468, which conveniently covered the dividend appropriation of $750,000 by Yellow Transit Company to its stockholders. The actual earned surplus figure at the close of 1948 was $7,468.

This "blood-letting" of December, 1948 was far removed indeed from the plan of careful reinvestment suggested by Nash. Nevertheless, the new group in control, headed by Robert C. Hardy as chairman of the board, was confident that the income-generating power of the growing company warranted the dividend appropriation.

Some of this optimism was undoubtedly cooled the next month; operations were completely halted for eleven days when severe weather throughout the operating area made the roads unsafe for travel. Loss for the month amounted to $31,607, and resumption of operations was slow and uncertain. Nash instituted a strict expense control plan in order to keep costs to an absolute minimum.

The poor showing in that one month demonstrated the thin operating margin of the truckline; a slight narrowing of the gap between revenues and expenses could produce a sharply reduced profit picture. Aware of this problem, Nash had become concerned by the price or rate increases sought by many carriers. Following the war, the costs of running a truckline advanced rapidly. In the face of rising costs, truckers were anxious to gain higher revenues, and one way was through price increases. However, if raising the price of truck carriage diverted traffic to other modes of transport, the price increase was self-defeating. In other words, for a price increase to be effective against rising cost levels, the volume of traffic had to grow, or at least remain constant.

TABLE 3
Wage Rates for Trucking Industry and Yellow Transit Company, 1945-49

	Industry			Yellow Transit		
Year	Total Revenue ($000)	Total Wages ($000)	Wages as a Per Cent of Revenue	Total Revenue ($000)	Total Wages ($000)	Wages as a Per Cent of Revenue
1945	$1,406,300	$ 711,588	50.6	$2,818	$1,346	47.8
1946	1,654,500	832,213	50.3	3,186	1,517	47.6
1947	2,213,600	1,086,878	49.1	3,822	1,869	48.9
1948	2,698,100	1,297,786	48.1	5,056	2,333	46.1
1949	2,911,200	1,478,890	50.8	5,077	2,525	49.7

SOURCE: *American Trucking Trends, 1959* and annual reports from president to chairman of the board.

The situation now, as viewed by Nash, was that, if further increases in rates were granted to trucklines, the shipping public would be tempted to follow one of two courses. First, traffic would return to the railroad if rates were sufficiently lower to offset possible service disadvantages. This alternative did not particularly concern Nash; he firmly believed that the flexibility of truckline service gave the trucks a great advantage, especially in small-lot, less-than-truckload business, which was the bulk of Yellow Transit's traffic. The second possibility was the use of private carriage, an alternative of major concern to Nash, who believed that high average common carrier rates made private trucking more attractive to shippers. Actually, a move to private carriage would have been somewhat complicated. A shipper would have to carefully analyze the volume, regularity, direction, and so forth of his traffic.

Since Yellow Transit had specialized in small-lot traffic and had traditionally been known as a high-rate carrier, the position taken by Nash following the 1948 rate increases caused some persons to wonder about the change of attitude. Nash explained that Yellow Transit was neither a high- nor a low-rate company; rather, its "higher" rates were coupled with "better" service to give shippers a superior product. This had also been the philosophy of A. J. Harrell.

The largest item of cost for a truckline is labor. Following World War II, the labor contracts that were negotiated substantially raised wage rates in the trucking industry. However, the trucking segment of transportation was also growing, and, as long as the two kept pace, all was well. Table 3 presents figures for the industry as a whole and for the Yellow Transit Company, using total truck revenues and total wages paid for trucking operations. The figures are interesting from at least two aspects. First, the total wage bills for the Yellow Transit Company, in comparison with revenues, were consistently lower than the same figures for the industry as a whole. This probably reflects the fact that wage rates were lower in the Kansas, Oklahoma, and Texas plains than in the more industrial northeast, where the majority of trucking was centered. Second, the trend of the Yellow Transit wage percentages followed Yellow Transit's revenue performance. The impressive gain from 1947 to 1948 was reflected in a significant 2.8 per cent drop in the wage figure, and the poor growth from 1948 to 1949 is clear from the 3.8 per cent gain in wages as a percentage of revenues.

The major problem in the labor area concerned overtime hours. Operations at the terminals were tightened in order to complete necessary freight handling within regular working hours. In addition, the acquisition of new equipment throughout the period reduced breakdown time. Drivers of disabled rigs received pay while waiting for repairs to restore the truck to a roadworthy condition. The entire problem was complicated by a reduction in the basic workweek, along with increased wages per hour worked, and, because Nash felt rather defenseless in fighting union demands, he attempted to meet the challenge through increased revenues.

One of the successful methods of increasing revenues that Yellow Transit had used in the past was expansion. During 1949, negotiations were completed with the Motor City Express, Inc. for a route from Chicago to Detroit. The cost to Yellow Transit for entrance into Detroit was $15,000, and the primary route was along former U.S. Highway 12, now Interstate 94, with an alternate via M 60. In addition to Detroit, such intermediate industrial centers as Kalamazoo, Battle Creek, and Jackson were added to the Yellow Transit system. Approval was granted by the ICC on Dec. 15, 1949.

A large number of accidents involving Yellow Transit drivers occurred following World War II, and, as the quality of the fleet was bettered by the purchase of new equipment, Nash noted that the safety record did not improve. As a result, according to the president's annual report to the chairman of the board for 1948, a campaign was inaugurated that year "to bring the company's record to a class that could be pointed to with pride." The first measure was a more careful screening of new drivers; the second was driver competition for safety awards in a contest sponsored by the American Trucking Association. The program was effective; Yellow Transit trucks were involved in 313 accidents during 1947, 277 in 1948, and 228 in 1949. Moreover, while the

TABLE 4
Operating Results for Trucking Industry and Yellow Transit Company, 1945-49

Year	Operating Ratio		Revenue per Vehicle Mile		Expense per Vehicle Mile	
	Yellow Transit	Industry	Yellow Transit	Industry	Yellow Transit	Industry
1945	98.8	99.8	.351	.337	.314	.344
1946	96.4	96.4	.370	.359	.321	.354
1947	96.5	95.3	.386	.393	.338	.384
1948	93.9	93.4	.416	.426	.357	.408
1949	97.2	94.7	.401	.426	.357	.414

SOURCE: Annual reports from president to chairman of the board; *Statistical Abstract of the United States 1943* and *1951* (Washington: U.S. Gov't Printing Office, 1943 and 1951).

absolute numbers were declining, the frequency as measured by accidents per 100,000 miles traveled was dropping even faster. In 1947, the frequency had been 2.26; by 1949 it was down to 1.61 accidents per 100,000 miles. The record was impressive enough to win Yellow Transit Company third place in the local and long-distance class over 12 million miles in the Fourteenth National Truck Safety Contest in 1948.

The year 1949 proved to be the last full year during which Evans A. Nash was president of Yellow Transit Company. The year was moderately successful in terms of profit, with a net income of $74,225, compared to $169,393 before dividends for 1948 and $87,775 for 1947. The consolidated figures for the Yellow Transit Company, Yellow Terminals, Inc., and the Yellow Equipment Company were: 1949, $200,502; 1948, $334,457; and 1947, $192,024. The board of directors of the Yellow Transit Company declared dividends of $81,000 in 1949, payable to the holding company, Yellow Transit Systems, Inc.

In Table 4, some operating results of the Yellow Transit Company are compared to the industry average. At the beginning of the period, Yellow Transit had enjoyed a higher revenue per vehicle mile than the average, but by 1949 the position had changed. In expenses, however, Yellow Transit stayed well below the industry average throughout the five-year period, but only in 1945 was the operating ratio superior to the average. In a word, the company was close to average—not a leader —during that period.

5 / JUST TWO SHORT YEARS

The middle part of the history of Yellow Transit closed with a two-year period beginning with the spring of 1950 and ending Oct. 27, 1952. During this short time, Yellow Transit Freight Lines, Inc. was founded in Indiana, the former Oklahoma-based Yellow Transit Company was merged into oblivion, Nash was removed from the presidency, and Yellow Transit filed for voluntary bankruptcy in the U.S. District Court for the Southern District of Indiana at Indianapolis. The careful work of twenty-five years was disastrously lost in two.

Although the first three months of 1949 had produced an operating loss of $4,333, the same quarter of 1950 generated income before taxes of $23,014. The revenue increase of $248,000 for the quarter led Nash to predict continued success to the board of directors. The six months from January to June, 1950 showed revenue of $2,828,400, compared with $2,428,700 for the previous year; income before taxes jumped from $25,680 to $68,786. The new group in control was convinced that a great era of profit was beginning.

Most members of the board were professional men entering their first big-time business venture. Unfortunately, the group was untutored in principles of economics and was inexperienced in the methods of successful business operations; they seemed to view gross revenue as the measure of business success and office decor as the test of personal achievement. Nash had contributed the necessary business acumen for profitable operation, and, until the spring of 1950, the new owners had been satisfied to follow his advice. At that time, the company's success provided the confidence the group needed to operate on its own.

THE NEW MANAGEMENT

The first change was proposed in the area of equipment. Plans were studied for an enlarged fleet of new business cars for salesmen and executives. The rolling fleet was to be updated on a grand scale and financed primarily through loans to the subsidiary companies. Fixed property was to be modernized, and new terminals were designed for several locations. Finally, the group considered schemes to move the headquarters from Oklahoma City to Dallas, the more glamorous financial and social center of the Southwest.

In 1950 Nash was forced out of the company; the charge was that he had failed in the performance of his office and that successful operation required his removal from active management. His eviction was not achieved without court action. In September, 1948, Robert C. Hardy, chairman of the board, had suggested both a salary increase and a longer contract period for Nash; the revised agreement was to run to September, 1953. When the new group pressured Nash out in 1950, he brought suit for breach of contract. The new owners sought to discredit Nash and prove the necessity for extensive modernization; Nash relied on the success of his administration in maintaining profitable operations. At the conclusion of a one-week trial at Oklahoma City, he was awarded full settlement of the broken contract. Yellow Transit's annual report to the Interstate Commerce Commission for 1951 contained a brief item that closed the case: "Schedule 8200.—Extraordinary Income Charges Award to E. A. Nash Including Legal Expenses $87,500."

With Nash removed as president, the new group moved ahead with its plans. Hardy became president, and in late September, 1950, the move to Dallas was initiated. The problems of the move that seemed most important to the new group centered on personal comfort rather than operations, and executive time was wasted on minor decisions. With top management concentrating on the superficial, it was but a matter of time until disaster struck.

The following paragraph is from a Sept. 30, 1950 letter written by the vice-president to the president:

On the matter of decoration, etc., I found that Montgomery Ward had no department in that area and so called in Sangers, which is a very excellent store and the oldest in Dallas. They have established a Department of Interior Design and have done several very excellent jobs. . . . They will do the corner office in the theme which you suggested, including a concealed but complete bar in what is now a closet at one end of the room. They will do the conference room in an appropriate style to match and then merely carpet Ed Horton's office.

Another problem concerned the selection of stationery:

On the general announcement which you worked out we have a low bid of $288.02 for lithographing on 15M of our letterhead in stock and an additional 10M which they will make up. . . . I presume that you will handle the layout for a new letterhead. . . . As I see this, there will be two or three types of letterheads carrying the new emblem: for example, Office of the Chairman, Office of the Vice President at Dallas and so on: Is this correct? . . . Bear in mind that the present correct full title on the ribbon, however, would be Yellow Transit *Co.* on the first segment and 'Freight Lines' on the right half of the banner. I think the simplicity of that pattern has a certain impact.

Late in 1950, further corporate juggling took place. A new corporation, Yellow Transit Freight Lines, Inc., was established on Dec. 22, 1950 in Indiana, and the old Oklahoma company was merged into the new concern effective Jan. 2, 1951. The five directors were Hardy, Edmund M. McCarthy, Vincent W. Westrup, and A. M. Mason, all of New York, and Theodore E. Dean of Dallas. Just before the change to Indiana, three subsidiary companies were founded in Delaware—the Dallas Equipment Company, Wilton Equipment Company, and Yellow Freight Lines Equipment, Inc. The number of corporate companies had grown to seven by the end of 1950, and in January, 1951 twenty-seven additional equipment and terminal companies had been established, bringing the number to thirty-four.

The action to establish a complicated corporate structure was motivated by a belief that great tax advantages would be available if the parent Yellow Transit Freight Lines leased equipment and terminals from subsidiaries. Perhaps this would have been the case if profits had been high, but 1950 was the last year of profitable operation under the new group; net profits were $112,655 for the consolidated system, as compared to $191,028 for 1949. Revenues in 1950 hit a new all-time high of $5,925,031 and gave the management group new hope.

During the first months of 1951, the addition of several subsidiaries brought the total number to fifty, including the Connecticut Development Corporation, holder of the 5,000 shares of the Yellow Transit Freight Lines, Inc. The complete list is shown in Table 5. At the same time, Hardy was involved in other corporate entanglements. According to *Poor's Register of Directors and Executives* for the 1947-50 period,

TABLE 5
Subsidiaries, End of 1951

	Date of Incorporation	State
Subsidiaries of Yellow Transit Freight Lines, Inc.	12/22/50	Indiana
Yellow Terminals, Inc.	3/10/45	Delaware
Yellow Equipment Co.	3/15/45	Illinois
Dallas Equipment Co.	11/27/50	Delaware
Wilton Equipment Co.	11/27/50	Delaware
Yellow Freight Lines Equipment, Inc.	12/ 6/50	Delaware
Indianapolis Yellow Equipment Corp.	1/ 2/51	Indiana
Indiana Yellow Equipment Corp.	1/24/51	Indiana
Yellow Trailer Equipment Corp.	1/26/51	Indiana
Yellow Equipment Co.	2/23/51	Indiana
Yellow Freight Lines Equipment, Inc.	4/23/51	Indiana
First Yellow Equipment Corp.	2/16/51	Indiana
Second Yellow Equipment Corp.	2/16/51	Indiana
Third Yellow Equipment Corp.	2/16/51	Indiana
Fourth Yellow Equipment Corp.	2/16/51	Indiana
Fifth Yellow Equipment Corp.	2/16/51	Indiana
Sixth Yellow Equipment Corp.	2/17/51	Indiana
Seventh Yellow Equipment Corp.	2/17/51	Indiana
Eighth Yellow Equipment Corp.	2/17/51	Indiana
Ninth Yellow Equipment Corp.	2/17/51	Indiana
Tenth Yellow Equipment Corp.	2/17/51	Indiana
Eleventh Yellow Equipment Corp.	4/17/51	Indiana
Twelfth Yellow Equipment Corp.	4/21/51	Indiana
Thirteenth Yellow Equipment Corp.	4/21/51	Indiana
Fourteenth Yellow Equipment Corp.	4/21/51	Indiana
Subsidiaries of Yellow Terminals, Inc.		
Amarillo Yellow Transist Terminals, Inc.	1/ 2/51	Texas
Ardmore Yellow Terminal, Inc.	1/ 2/51	Oklahoma
Austin Yellow Terminal, Inc.	1/ 2/51	Texas
Baxter Springs Yellow Terminal, Inc.	1/ 2/51	Kansas
Cicero Avenue Yellow Terminal, Inc.	1/ 2/51	Illinois
Dallas Yellow Terminal, Inc.	1/ 2/51	Texas
Detroit Yellow Terminal, Inc.	1/ 2/51	Michigan
Evansville Yellow Terminal, Inc.	1/ 2/51	Indiana
Fort Worth Yellow Terminal, Inc.	1/ 2/51	Texas
Houston Yellow Terminal, Inc.	1/ 2/51	Texas
Indianapolis Yellow Terminal, Inc.	1/ 2/51	Indiana
Joplin Yellow Terminal, Inc.	1/ 2/51	Missouri
Kansas City Yellow Terminal, Inc.	1/ 2/51	Missouri
Louisville Yellow Terminal, Inc.	1/ 2/51	Kentucky
Mattoon Yellow Terminal, Inc.	1/ 2/51	Illinois
Muskogee Yellow Terminal, Inc.	1/ 2/51	Oklahoma
Oklahoma City Yellow Terminal, Inc.	1/ 2/51	Oklahoma
St. Louis Yellow Terminal, Inc.	1/ 2/51	Missouri
San Antonio Yellow Terminal, Inc.	1/ 2/51	Texas
Springfield Yellow Terminal, Inc.	1/ 2/51	Missouri
Tulsa Yellow Terminal, Inc.	1/ 2/51	Oklahoma
Vincennes Yellow Terminal, Inc.	1/ 2/51	Indiana
Wichita Falls Yellow Terminal, Inc.	1/ 2/51	Texas
Wichita Yellow Terminal, Inc.	1/ 2/51	Kansas

he was director of twenty other companies and president of two more, in addition to Yellow Transit and subsidiaries. He was listed as president of American Steel & Pump Corp. and Barium Steel and Pump Corp., and director of Fitzsimons Steel Company, Inc.; Oklahoma Steel Castings Co., Inc.; Clyde Iron Works, Inc.; Erie Bolt & Nut Company; Barium Steel & Forge Company; Geometric Stamping Company; Globe Forge, Inc.; Kermath Manufacturing Co.; Kermath Manufacturing Co. of Canada, Ltd.; Detroit Steel Castings Co.; Central Iron & Steel Co.; Wiley Manufacturing Co.; Porcelain Steels Corp.; Republic Industries, Inc.; Twentieth Century Press, Inc.; American Steel and Copper Industries, Inc.; Cole Industries, Inc.; Federal Electric Products Co.; Switch, Panel & Control Division, Inc.; and Wm. Wurdack Electric Manufacturing Co.

By 1952, Hardy was no longer connected with any of these companies and was not listed in *Poor's*.

The increasing gross revenues in 1951 served to reassure the group, and more terminals were built or leased throughout the system. New equipment was also acquired by lease, and the net operating rent figure jumped from $258,868 in 1950 to $1,021,245 in 1951, according to the annual reports for those years, suggesting extravagant leasing. Total operating revenues during the period grew by $2,000,000, but operating expenses jumped $1,800,000, and total expenses advanced $2,900,000.

Another sharp increase occurred in administrative and general expense; the total had risen from $385,398, in 1950 to $693,305, in 1951. The new group voted themselves handsome salaries and large bonuses. Moreover, the number of employees increased from 772 in 1950 to 1,096 in 1951. On a percentage basis, these figures represented gains of 34.4 per cent in revenues, 49.9 per cent in total expenses, and 41.9 per cent in the number of employees in a one-year period!

By late 1951, it was obvious that Yellow Transit was in trouble. The group in control decided that a central office in Indianapolis would help establish a more stable company since Yellow Transit had been maintaining its general office at Dallas and its corporate headquarters in New York. Indiana was chosen because so many subsidiaries were incorporated there, and because the group felt that purchasing all license plates in one state would reduce the total bills.[1] In January,

[1]The original locations considered were Evansville, Vincennes, and Indianapolis. Evansville was rejected because the cost of repairs would have been prohibitive; although the record does not so state, apparently the rejuvenation of a terminal building was considered. Vincennes was unacceptable because it was not a scheduled airline stop.

1952, executive offices were rented. The contract was to run for one year at a rental of $6,600; Yellow Transit also contracted for $8,119 in alterations and decoration.

On Dec. 11, 1951, the creditors placed four men on the board of Yellow Transit. On that same day, according to the corporate minutes, "it was the consensus of the members of the Board that it was absolutely necessary to cause an independent investigation of the operational affairs of this company so as to effectuate a plan of successful and profitable operation." In response, Earl Winters of Detroit was hired on Jan. 24, 1952, but action had come too late. Bankruptcy appeared to be the only alternative. On Feb. 29, 1952, the company filed a voluntary petition under Chapter XI of the Bankruptcy Act. The petition for the appointment of a receiver dated March 4, 1952, succinctly stated the case:

> The petitioners have no confidence in the ability and business judgement of the present management of the debtor. This business, which in 1949 had an operating income of $326,003.28 and in 1950 had an operating income of $193,445.57, has been so mismanaged as to cause an operational loss during the last year of the sum of $621,868.72.
>
> That this loss was occasioned by the improvident leasing and purchase of various equipment and terminal facilities, in an increase in rental expense of from $49,284.77 in 1950 to $209,645.29 in 1951, and by the inordinately high salaries which were paid to the management officials. Some of said salaries were paid retroactively. In 1950 administrative expenses were $385,398.20 and in 1951 those expenses had skyrocketed to $693,305.06.[2]

On March 7, John K. Rickles was appointed referee, and for the next eight months the company was run under the guidance of the court. (On March 20, Hardy resigned as president, and the company had no elected president until April 29, when A. W. Guilland took office.) The breakdown within the company was ably expressed by A. E. Robert Friedman, co-counsel for the debtor:

> There existed a complete lack of confidence within the organization and among the top officials, particularly among the board of directors.
>
> There was bitter animosity between various factions. Mrs. Porter and her children, the survivors of the late Arlington W. Porter, who had purchased, owned, and controlled all of the stock of Yellow Transit Freight Lines, Inc.,

---

[2]Transcript of Docket No. 9816 in Bankruptcy, Indianapolis Division, Southern District of Indiana.

were bitter about the whole situation and felt that they were the victims of colossal incompetence.[3]

The total debt of the company amounted to $3,323,129.29, broken down as follows: priority claims (taxes), $211,026.23; secured indebtedness, $2,398,166.28; and unsecured indebtedness, $713,936.78. The petition for bankruptcy included all companies of the Yellow Transit Freight Lines, Inc. Referee Rickles, in his final report, stated: "The corporate structure of the debtor corporation was rather complex. The petition as filed sought to place under the jurisdiction of the court not only the debtor but forty-eight (48) of its wholly owned subsidiaries." Problems of straightening out the complexities were complicated by the faulty records of the companies:

> At the commencement of these proceedings the minutes of Yellow Transit Freight Lines, Inc., and all of its subsidiary corporations were in a deplorable state. Organizational minutes were incomplete, many signatures were missing, virtually no minutes beyond organization-mention were ever transcribed.[4]

Slowly, however, the situation was improved. Leases were considered and adjusted where possible. In one case, according to the docket transcript, "counsel also negotiated cancellation of a very expensive lease of new terminal property being constructed in Detroit, Michigan, which was far beyond debtor's needs."

MORE NEW OWNERS

The failure of Yellow Transit naturally attracted the attention of the trucking industry, and several groups and companies approached the court with inquiries about possible purchase. Included were Associated Transport, Roadway Express, Ziffrin, Interstate Motor Freight, and a Texas group headed by Clint Murchison, who promptly disclaimed interest, saying he knew nothing about the trucking industry. Navajo Freight Lines, Inc. offered an outright purchase of the outstanding shares plus a loan of some $300,000. Although the offer was accepted by Yellow Transit and signed on March 19, 1952, according to the docket transcript, the amount of cash to be given was far too low, and the agreement was mutually cancelled.

Finally, on April 29, 1952, an agreement was signed between Yellow

---

[3]Transcript of Docket No. 9816.
[4]Schedule J, Transcript of Docket No. 9816.

Transit Freight Lines, Inc. and George E. Powell of Kansas City, Mo. Powell agreed to make $750,000 available to Yellow Transit, providing several conditions were met. First, the capital structure was to be altered to provide for authority to issue 100,000 shares of common stock and 6,600 shares of preferred. (Subsequently, the number of preferred shares authorized was reduced to 4,900.) The preferred shares were to be issued to former common shareholders, and a portion of the new common stock was to be issued to Powell or his nominees, with the remainder of the shares covered by a restricted stock option plan through which the Powell group could acquire the balance. Second, each of the management personnel of the company was to sign a release of all claims and demands against Yellow Transit and to resign. Third, Powell was to be appointed general manager of the company. Several other provisions were included in the agreement, involving repayment of the $750,000 loan (subsequently reduced to $675,000), the payment of fees and expenses arising from the bankruptcy proceedings, and the methods of meeting creditor demands. On May 1, the referee in bankruptcy agreed to the plan, and Powell was appointed general manager of Yellow Transit Freight Lines, Inc.

Concurrently, the truckline operations had to be put in order, the wreckage of the previous management had to be cleared away (this involved creditor approval), and Interstate Commerce Commission sanction had to be obtained. Powell's ability as general manager was demonstrated by the following figures:

	Operating Revenues	Operating Expenses	Profit (Loss)
March, 1952	$662,281	$694,906	($32,625)
October, 1952	663,756	638,204	25,552

The ICC studied carefully the plan for the rejuvenation of Yellow Freight Lines and checked the qualifications of Powell and his associates. The changeover was approved on Sept. 2, 1952. One of the requirements of the commission was corporate simplification. W. L. Fulton of the securities section of the ICC stated that the truckline had "a flock of corporations" and he knew of no other instance that had come before the commission in which so many were involved.

Creditor approval of the reorganization came on Oct. 7, 1952. The plan for creditor payments as listed in the records of the court was as follows:

All taxes (class 1 debts) to be paid in full upon confirmation.
All adjudicated and compromised claims (class 2) to be paid in full on confirmation.

All unsecured claims under $500 (class 3) to be paid in full on confirmation.

All unsecured claims over $500 (class 4) to be paid 10% in cash upon confirmation, the balance to be represented by debtor's notes to the respective creditors, payable in twelve monthly installments.

All unliquidated claims except cargo claims (class 5) when liquidated after confirmation to be paid directly by the debtor, 10% in cash and 90% in twelve monthly installments.

All unliquidated cargo claims (class 6) to be paid forthwith upon liquidation.[5]

On Oct. 27, 1952, Yellow Transit was released from federal court jurisdiction, and the company came under the control of its new management. The second period in the history of Yellow Transit had ended.

[5]Transcript of Docket No. 9816.

6 | A YEAR CAN MAKE A LOT OF DIFFERENCE

"The Yellow Transit Freight Lines, Inc., 18 East Seventeenth Street, Kansas City, Missouri, was released from federal court jurisdiction October 27 and the following day announced the election of new officers and directors, headed by George E. Powell, Sr., . . . as president."[1]

The six months preceding this notice had been marked by legal and operational turmoil. Powell had been appointed general manager on May 1, 1952, at the height of the managerial difficulties. Although the day-to-day operations of the truckline had continued, the problems were thorny. The complete breakdown of confidence at the top affected all levels of the organization, and workers wondered whether their jobs were secure. Since Yellow Transit had been forced to suspend maintenance for lack of funds, equipment was in poor condition, and trucks were used until major breakdowns occurred. For a short period in March, 1952, some even operated with expired license plates.

The appointment of Powell was regarded with enthusiasm by company employees; formerly vice-chairman of Riss and Company, then one of the nation's largest motor carriers, Powell was known as an able manager. At the time of the appointment, George E. Powell, Jr. was named as controller.

The intricate corporate structure created legal problems that proved to be a major test for the Powell administration. Kenneth E. Midgley, a Kansas City attorney who was one of the original group of Powell

[1]*Kansas City Star*, Oct. 28, 1952.

associates, handled the legal aspects and gradually found a path through the entanglements. Operations were surveyed throughout the system and changes made. Progress was slow. During May, June, July, and August, the company continued to show a deficit, but in September, 1952, a "black ink" balance again appeared and stayed—with the exception of two months during the following winter.

The offices of the company were moved from Dallas to Kansas City, Mo., Powell's home. The operational setup was divided into two divisions with superintendents in charge. The southern division was headquartered at Dallas and the northern division at St. Louis. At the time, some questions were raised about the separation of the corporate offices from the operational centers of the system. In terms of traffic flow through a particular city, St. Louis, Baxter Springs, or possibly Dallas would have been a more strategic location than Kansas City. Moreover, the traditional concept of both Yellow Transit and the industry in general had been that of a one-man operation, which required on-the-spot knowledge. The Powells, therefore, broke with precedents in the selection of corporate headquarters—and did so knowingly. Their philosophy was oriented more toward standard business practices, that is, appointment of operations people to run the line without interference from their superiors. In other words, the Powells assumed full management, but delegated authority and responsibility for specific segments of the operation. Some personnel changes resulted early in 1953 when longtime employees found it difficult to adjust to the reorganization. As a result of resignations, top management soon became "Powell appointed," a change that, in time, was felt throughout the entire organization.

Powell was born at Linneus, Mo. and attended Chillicothe Business College. He worked for the Baltimore Bank of Kansas City from 1921 to 1941, when he left his position as vice-president to become executive vice-president of the Trader's National Bank of Kansas City until 1947.

As a banker, he became intrigued with the challenge offered in the transportation business when he was called in to help several companies out of financial scrapes. So, when Richard Riss, president of the far-flung trucking empire known as Riss and Company, Inc. offered him the presidency of the Riss organization, Powell didn't hesitate long before accepting. Those who worked with him at Riss claim Powell knew as much about the trucking business after five years as many veterans knew after 25.[2]

[2]Jack Thiessen, "Trucking's Full-Grown Infant," *Business on Wheels* (Akron: The Goodyear Tire and Rubber Company, Inc., 1954), p. 10.

In some ways, the transportation business and the banking business are similar, and Powell's experience gave him considerable advantage at Yellow Transit. First, he was familiar with the kind of financial problems the company faced. Second, he had the successful banker's finesse and knowledge of the needs of other businesses, which proved useful in transforming Yellow Transit into a market-oriented, service-minded truckline.

PERSONNEL CHANGES

Purchase of the truckline provided Powell with his first opportunity to run his own company. Among his objectives was the desire to make the company a good place to work and to provide employees with opportunity for advancement and success. He became known for his honesty of purpose, forthrightness in dealings, and high ethical standards. These were the principles on which Powell built his life and his company.

> When a company is re-organized, it is assumed that some alterations will be made in the executive structure. By comparison, Powell put up a whole new building with virgin timber. And he gathered around him what must have seemed to older heads, the strangest conglomeration of backgrounds and professions ever to serve as the executive framework of a trucking company. . . . In looking back, the senior Powell admits that after he selected his administrative staff there were probably many veteran truckers who thought he would be better off in a nice, quiet room with padded walls and barred windows. They foresaw Yellow Transit back on the auction block within another year.[3]

Powell's new administrative staff did have questionable qualifications for running a trucking business, but Powell was interested in aggressive, service-minded department heads with business know-how. The functional division of the work was traditional, however; sales and operations were completely separated.

For the position of vice-president-traffic and sales, Powell selected Hugh W. Coburn, a twenty-five-year airline veteran and former vice-president of Mid-Continent Airlines. It was his task to assemble the sales crew for the new Yellow Transit. On the operations side, Powell brought in his son, George E. Powell, Jr., who had attended Northwestern University and at 26 had been secretary-treasurer of Riss and Company.

[3]"Trucking's Full-Grown Infant," p. 10.

George E. Powell

He became chief of both the operations and the accounting departments. The three key operating men reporting to the younger Powell were also freshly recruited. The post of superintendent of terminals was filled by David D. Padgett, who had joined Yellow Transit as Kansas City terminal manager about the time of the Powell takeover. He had been in sales and operational capacities with other trucklines for eleven years. William R. Riley, hired as superintendent of maintenance, had been a branch manager and engineer with a truck manufacturer. Robert J. Leary left a position in the frozen food storage and distribution business to become superintendent of transportation. The fate of Yellow Transit was now in the hands of young executives. (At that time, the ages of these men ranged from 26 to 29, and seasoned truckers were startled by such obvious lack of experience.) Rounding out the top personnel were two people retained from the previous organization— L. E. Tomlinson, a Yellow Transit employee from the days of A. J. Harrell, as rate man, and Harold H. Edwards, the young treasurer, a graduate of Oklahoma City University, who stayed on in Dallas.

Somewhat later, three additional men were employed, each of whom influenced the development of the company. Mark Robeson, another banker turned trucker, who had been first vice-president of Riss in charge of sales and overseer of that company's equipment program, joined Yellow Transit as government traffic representative, an especially important post then because of the Korean conflict. Donald L. McMorris

George E. Powell, Jr.

joined Yellow Transit in 1954 as controller; he had previously been auditor, controller, and treasurer of Riss and Company. Both Robeson and McMorris were University of Kansas graduates. Finally, Donald E. Sable joined Yellow Transit in 1953 as district sales manager at Dallas.

To this group fell the responsibility and opportunity of remaking Yellow Transit into the fine truckline it once had been. After a few changes, the members of the board of directors, charged with the overall destiny of the company, were George E. Powell, George E. Powell, Jr., Hugh W. Coburn, Lester H. Brickman, George L. Williams, Kenneth E. Midgley, and A. E. Robert Friedman. The first three were both directors and full-time officers of the company; Brickman and Williams were members of the original group that Powell had assembled to finance the takeover of the company. Midgley, the chief legal adviser, became secretary of Yellow Transit Freight Lines while retaining his position with the Kansas City law firm today known as Swanson, Midgley, Jones, Eager and Gangwere. Born in Salt Lake City, Midgley graduated from the University of Utah and The University of Michigan law school. Finally, Friedman was the representative of the preferred shares that had been issued to the common stockholders of record before the reorganization.

MASTERING THE OPERATION

Changes in activities, as well as in personnel, took place during the months following reorganization. First, the matter of payments to creditors was undertaken as stipulated in the reorganization proceedings. Checks paying all taxes, adjudicated and compromised claims, and unsecured claims under $500 were mailed immediately following the Oct. 27, 1952 release from federal court jurisdiction. Checks for 10 per cent of the amount of claims in excess of $500 were sent out; the balances of these accounts were to be paid in twelve monthly installments and were to be represented by Yellow Transit Freight Lines notes payable. The total amount of these notes was $328,203. By October, 1953, these obligations had been paid in full.

Long-term obligations not included in the current liabilities also had to be met. Including interest, these obligations totaled $886,297 in 1953. Schedules of some of the larger accounts are shown in Table 6. The first year had made considerable headway in debt reduction.

In the application for change in the capital structure of Yellow Transit Freight Lines, Inc., which was approved by the Interstate Commerce Commission Sept. 2, 1952, the Powell group had stated that it intended to reduce the number of subsidiary corporations to not more than two. Good business procedure required careful processing of dissolution of the many companies because of tax considerations. The Powell group had acquired forty-nine companies in all; by the end of 1952, six of the subsidiaries, which had been nonfunctioning and possessed no assets other than original capital, were dissolved, and sixteen of the equipment companies were merged into the Indiana Yellow Equipment Corporation. In the early months of 1953, seventeen additional terminal companies were dissolved, and by the end of 1953 the number of companies was down to six—Yellow Transit Freight Lines, Inc. plus five subsidiaries. In approximately one year, the forty-nine companies had been reduced to six.

Equipment, naturally, had suffered during the period when no cash was available for repairs, and ". . . Powell found, somewhat to his surprise, that more than half of the 940 units were less than three years old. The previous management had embarked on a huge replacement program, but had de-emphasized the maintenance program as a result."[4]

_____

[4] "Trucking's Full-Grown Infant," p. 11.

TABLE 6

Schedule of Selected Accounts for Yellow Transit and Subsidiaries, 1953

1953	Fruehauf Trailer Company	White Motor Company	Republic National Bank	Texas Bank and Trust Company
January	$ 29,666	$ 16,150	$ 5,761	$ 3,082
February	30,646	16,150	5,737	3,068
March	32,117	16,150	5,624	3,053
April	32,116	16,150	5,687	3,039
May	32,116	16,150	5,634	3,025
June	32,116	15,205	5,637	3,010
July	32,116	14,176	5,586	2,996
August	32,116	14,176	5,588	2,982
September	32,116	14,176	5,563	2,967
October	37,298	16,104	5,514	3,703
November	37,298	16,104	5,513	3,689
December	37,298	16,104	5,466	3,675
Totals	*$397,027*	*$186,801*	*$67,316*	*$38,294*

*Details may not add to totals because of rounding.

SOURCE: Financial statement of Yellow Transit Freight Lines, Inc. and subsidiary companies, Dec. 31, 1952.

The inherited equipment was powered with gasoline engines, which require relatively more maintenance than diesel engines. The superintendent of maintenance promptly set up a system of periodic checks on equipment at five central maintenance centers—Dallas, Baxter Springs, Chicago, St. Louis, and Oklahoma City. The Yellow Transit fleet was soon back in top shape, and, as a result, equipment downtime and failures dropped substantially.

Yellow Transit's terminals had also been modernized under the previous administration, and about half were less than five years old. Nevertheless, substantial economies were realized by realigning procedures and scheduling inbound and outbound traffic more carefully. Some of the realigning was made possible by the new sales emphasis that was gradually instituted. In January, 1952, the previous management had instructed the salesmen to accept all freight; the company needed all the revenue it could get. This instruction, plus deterioration of service, meant that quality traffic—once the major part of the company's consist[5]—ceased to move by Yellow Transit. Therefore, although revenues remained about the same, more work was required to

---

[5]"Consist" has a precise meaning and pronunciation in transportation jargon. In trucking it refers to the tonnage being hauled.

TABLE 7
Comparison of Operating Results, 1952 and 1953

	1952	1953
Operating revenue	$7,482,728	$8,047,771
Operating expenses	7,648,758	7,680,413
Operating income or loss	−$166,030	$367,358
Other income	....	146,075
Other deductions	251,498	117,570
Totals	−$417,528	$395,863

gain it; a profit cut was the inevitable result. In 1952, 8,373 truckload and 680,016 less-than-truckload shipments had been carried to produce operating revenues of $7,482,728. In 1953, 8,979 truckload and 501,-659 less-than-truckload shipments brought in revenues of $8,047,770. The quality of traffic was clearly on the upswing. An important contributing factor was the decision to abandon over 100 agency stations that had been set up by the previous management. Control of the agents was virtually impossible and the return marginal, so the agency agreements were terminated late in 1952.

The Yellow Transit system that had been put together piecemeal by A. J. Harrell consisted of both intrastate and interstate operating rights in many locations. The Powell management group decided to compete for both quality traffic and the long-haul interstate business, and undertook the streamlining of operating authorities. Several legs of the system's intrastate rights, such as that between Tulsa and Oklahoma City, were sold, an action that both simplified the system and provided needed funds.

In virtually every aspect of the company, new systematic methods were introduced. The changes were small and numerous, rather than sweeping. The metamorphosis is perhaps best illustrated by a comparison of the operating results for 1953 and 1952. Table 7 presents the major figures on a consolidated basis.

About that time, as a part of Yellow Transit's sales campaign, shippers were sent a folder featuring a gangling, adolescent girl on the cover and a curvaceous, blond bathing beauty inside. The caption said simply, "A year can make a lot of difference." The operating results of 1953 justified the caption, and, in the succeeding years, equally impressive gains were registered. The chapters that follow will discuss these years from a functional rather than a chronological perspective.

7 | ROLLING DOWN THE ROAD

To the casual observer, a truckline is simply a vehicle on the highway, or possibly a shed-like terminal. These are only two of the many physical considerations that make up the production line of a trucking company. This chapter concerns the tools of production and improvements in the physical plant of Yellow Transit Freight Lines after 1952, the third period of its history.

At the time of the takeover of Yellow Transit by the current management group, few trucklines had matured to the point where long-run planning was an important part of the managerial duties. Most of them were small businesses where day-to-day operations absorbed all the working hours. Indeed, before 1950, the classification by the Interstate Commerce Commission of a Class I motor carrier was one having annual gross revenues of $100,000 or more. In 1949, 2,728 carriers were in that category. The 1950 revision raised the base revenue figure to $200,000, and, by 1952, a total of 2,361 carriers were classified in the first grouping.[1]

Perhaps more significant than size, however, was the nature of the managements of the trucklines. Many lines had grown from one-man operations into larger businesses, just as Yellow Transit had, but many had retained the "one sparkplug" type of organization. The single manager might be well qualified in many respects, but usually his long suit was an acute business sense that carried him through, rather than

---

[1]American Trucking Associations, Inc., *American Trucking Trends. 1959* (Washington, D.C.: American Trucking Associations, Inc., 1959), p. 7.

extensive knowledge in the area that has become known as scientific management.

The success of many of these companies was the result of the know-how of the early truckline leaders, but the dissolutions and mergers of recent years also document the lack of management depth that existed in small concerns. Yellow Transit, of course, had traditionally been a company with one man at the helm, and throughout its early years had been blessed with able men—first A. J. Harrell, then Evans A. Nash. The operation was conservative and slow growing, but this program did not suit the investors who owned the company in the late forties. This group chose to make extensive and expensive improvements in equipment and facilities without the necessary planning and long-run considerations that must precede such major overhauls. Some decisions seem to have been based on show, others on incomplete knowledge, and virtually all on the philosophy that "bigger" equals "better." The result, as we have seen, was the ruin of the company.

The Powell management established order; almost immediately, budgets were established for every department of the company. With budgets came control, and good control required planning (both short and long run), an element that had been missing at Yellow Transit. This chapter will trace the planning of specific aspects of the truckline over the years.

ROLLING STOCK

Yellow Transit vehicles traditionally had been gasoline powered and were assigned to specific drivers charged with the care of the vehicle. This scheme had been developed when repair parts and tool costs were relatively more important than labor. This plan kept maintenance costs down, and equipment was in use for several years; any new equipment that had to be purchased was immediately assigned to a certain driver. The major difficulty with the plan was inflexibility—when the assigned driver was not working, the truck was not being used. This arrangement also caused clusters of equipment to move in certain areas only—those where the drivers lived—not around the system in its entirety. Therefore, several repair shops had to be located around the system. The terminals at St. Louis, Chicago, Indianapolis, Louisville, Kansas City, Oklahoma City, Dallas, and Baxter Springs were equipped to repair road equipment, in addition to performing maintenance services for local pickup and delivery fleets.

Of the fleet of trucks inherited by the new management, 38 per cent were 1950 models or older; their repair was undertaken in the shops. Such work was expensive, and not until June, 1953 were the maintenance expenses down to the budgeted level. Nevertheless, returning the owned fleet to top condition was considered less costly than major replacement, although some trailers were replaced in 1953 and 1954. Improving profits generated funds on a month-to-month basis that could be applied to strict preventive maintenance, and, throughout 1953, 1954, and early 1955, this program brought the rolling stock into first-class shape. As the miles and years accumulated, replacements were going to be required.

As early as Jan. 21, 1954, diesel power was suggested in the meetings of the board of directors of Yellow Transit, and by early 1955 extensive studies were underway to determine the best equipment for the operation. George Powell, Jr., then vice-president-operations, and W. R. Riley, superintendent of maintenance at the time, were the two principals in the study.

Among the many factors considered was weight. They needed a lightweight tractor that would pull the new high-cube trailers. Other factors were ease of maintenance and, particularly, accessibility to the engine compartment. (At this point, the CBE (cab-beside-engine) design began to look attractive.) In addition, it was felt that good visibility and driver comfort were extremely important. Availability of parts and service was considered. In short, everything affecting maintenance cost, including labor, was considered along with the operating needs.

With their requirements set down, Powell and Riley began talking to other fleet operators and studying their experience with various types of equipment. In the course of their study, it began to appear that a switch from gasoline-powered equipment to diesel power would give them the best answers to the question, 'What type of power equipment is best suited to our operation?'[2]

After a study of every facet of equipment needs and costs, a switch to diesel power was recommended. An extensive analysis of the specific operating requirements of Yellow Transit was made by the equipment staff of the Kenworth Motor Truck Corporation of Seattle, and eventually 200 tractors "were custom-engineered and manufactured for Yellow Transit by Kenworth. . . . The cab-beside-engine design was

[2]"Why Did Yellow Transit Go Diesel?" *Diesel Power* (December, 1955), pp. 31-32.

selected for maximum driver visibility, low weight, short over-all length and ease of access to the engine for maintenance. Extensive use of aluminum, plus the CBE design, have resulted in low tractor chassis weight for increased payloads."[3]

The power plant in the new tractors was a Cummins Turbodiesel engine. The new engines were rated 175 horsepower at 2,500 revolutions per minute and were considered high in power compared to weight. "Horsepower at the wheels, goal of every truckline operator, and decidedly different from theoretical or brake horsepower, went up more than 40 per cent. . . . The new tractors deliver an average of 134 hp at the wheels in comparison with 80 to 90 hp with the old units."[4]

In all, 250 gasoline-powered tractors were replaced by the 200 new Kenworth-Cummins rigs. At the same time, the entire fleet of trailers was replaced by 400 new volume-van trailers, 35 feet in length. The new trailers, manufactured by the Fruehauf Company of Detroit, featured aluminum bodies. The old trailers contained 1,700 cubic feet and the new ones, 2,100; the cubic area of the Yellow Transit trailer fleet was thereby increased about 30 per cent. The total purchase of tractors and trailers was one of the largest equipment orders in the trucking industry at that time. The move also indicated the forward thinking of the "new" Yellow Transit. During the next few years, additional tractors of the same type were acquired until the total reached 350, and Yellow Transit became well-known for its "telephone booth" cabs. The uniformity of the entire fleet added a marketing dimension, also, in that observers could readily identify a Yellow Transit vehicle.

The system of assigning a rig to each driver was abandoned at this time in favor of a "slip seat" or relay plan. A single tractor-trailer combination could make an entire run, for example, from Detroit to Dallas, and the driver, not the tractor, was switched. Utilization of equipment was increased because any one tractor could be in use at any time, and scheduling was made more flexible.

Trucking tradition maintained that drivers accustomed to gasoline powered rigs would not drive diesel equipment. Expensive training schools were considered a necessity to such a change; otherwise, new drivers had to be hired.

[3]*Transport Topics* (Aug. 22, 1955), p. 2.

[4]L. H. Houck, "Yellow Transit Goes All Diesel," *Diesel Progress* (January, 1956), p. 26.

Driver transition at Yellow Transit was accomplished with record smoothness, with personnel and terminal managers turning in continuing reports of pleased and enthusiatic drivers, who have suddenly discovered they can handle bigger loads with less work and with better visibility, and that turbocharged engines are more flexible in heavy traffic, with faster schedules possible over the road and less shifting on hills.[5]

Through careful planning and training before the change to diesels, Yellow Transit had been able to gain operating advantages with a minimum of driver dissatisfaction. Each driver was carefully instructed by professional driver trainers from the Cummins Engine Company.

About this time, maintenance facilities were consolidated in the central location of the one-time cow town, Baxter Springs, Kan. Use of the relay system meant that each tractor could be routed to Baxter Springs for repairs and maintenance when required.

Changing a terminal garage with five mechanics to a consolidated system repair shop with 25 mechanics, and assuming service on 216 over-the-road tractors and all associated equipment, are ingredients composing a fair-sized problem.

This is the problem that faced Yellow Transit Freight Lines, Kansas City, Missouri, when it changed from gasoline rigs to new Kenworth cab-beside-engine, diesel-powered tractors, eliminated 10 road shops, and established a headquarters maintenance shop at Baxter Springs, Kansas, where it has become the biggest business in town.[6]

The old shop at Baxter Springs was totally changed; new and different equipment was required for diesel maintenance, and the location of the equipment within the shop had to be altered. Although the existing building contained adequate floor space, the flow of traffic was reversed. A pit, which was not useful in the new layout, was converted into a 4,500-gallon storage vat for drained oil. The top was covered over with concrete, making a smooth floor in the garage, and the oil was sold for use on gravel roads or for crude heating plants designed to burn waste oil.

Because diesel engines tend to be noisy, many truckline maintenance shops have separate buildings for the use of dynamometers, devices

[5]"Yellow Transit Goes All Diesel," p. 27.
[6]L. H. Houck, "Yellow Transit Swaps 10 Shops for 1," *Commercial Car Journal* (September, 1956), p. 66.

that check the operation of running engines. This arrangement is often unhandy, and Yellow Transit solved the problem at Baxter Springs by installing the dynamometer near the exit door. An overhead exhaust removal system carried most of the noise away. The work flow was thus simplified; a tractor approved for service by the dynamometer could immediately move out for the "road-run lineup," while rejected units could be driven around the building and back inside for whatever work was indicated.

Substantial savings were possible with the central maintenance shop. Fewer mechanics, helpers, and laborers were required, and the investment in tools and equipment was reduced. The centralized parts inventory and the uniformity of equipment not only reduced the investment in parts, but also improved the availability of needed items.

For the next several years, a preventive maintenance program with the highest standards was instituted at Yellow Transit. Fleet additions were of the same Kenworth-Cummins equipment, thereby retaining uniformity. Major overhauls were undertaken as necessary, and the Kenworths were retained until 1961. At that time, Yellow Transit leased 200 White tractors on a thirty-month basis to replace a similar number of Kenworths. In 1962, another replacement took place, this time with GMC's. In 1963, the leased Whites were purchased and traded for fifty Whites, fifty Fords, fifty GMC's, and fifty Kenworths. Although this action appeared to reverse the standardization attempt of the 1955 switch, the ever-changing cost picture had altered the variables to the extent that a revised equipment policy was called for.

Standardization of equipment had helped reduce the substantial maintenance bill, but, as the equipment aged, repair costs went up. The next step in maintenance reduction was to replace the tractors before major repairs were necessary, and this was the prime factor behind the plan of trading approximately every two years. The purchase of the 1961 Whites was the first experiment with this policy. About the time that major work on them was necessary, Yellow Transit turned them in; since then, the company has performed no major overhaul work whatsoever. The parts inventories have dropped, and the funds once tied up have been made available for other purposes—probably for investment in the new equipment. The maintenance labor force has been reduced, thereby effecting further savings in direct labor. In other words, Yellow Transit has substituted capital for labor in the equipment line, similar to the action of manufacturing companies when they purchase labor-saving machinery.

Trailers have also been kept new through trades. For example, in 1959, the company swapped its fleet of 35-foot trailers for new 40-foot trailers. Then just three years later, the trailer fleet was again replaced by 767 new trailers. One of the side benefits of the frequent replacement of the equipment has been the fine appearance of Yellow Transit equipment; from the days of A. J. Harrell, clean and shiny trucks have characterized the fleet. A second advantage has been the ability to own several kinds of equipment without the bad features of a non-standardized fleet, such as parts problems. Mixture alone was of no particular benefit, but the freedom to purchase from several manufacturers gave the company an opportunity to engage in the great unsung aspect of doing business—reciprocity.

Since the investment in tires by a truckline is substantial, time and care are given to the stock. Most trucklines recapped tires, but Yellow Transit maintained that recapping did not pay because the rubber separated from the rest of the tire. The company felt the return on the dollar invested in recapping was less than on the dollar spent on new tires; although the total investment in new tires was greater, the rate of return was sufficiently higher to warrant the larger investment.

New tires were bought and stamped with a company serial number that was kept on file in the perpetual inventory at Baxter Springs. This inventory also listed the location of each tire. The new tires remained on the wheels until the cords appeared or some other major malfunction developed; they were then removed and sold for scrap. If a failure occurred on the road, a man was sent out from one of the repair stations located throughout the system. These were usually service stations on the routes traveled by Yellow Transit trucks. Spare tires were not carried on the trucks—the loss rate was too great, and spares tied up capital needed elsewhere.

At one time, the company did have a rotation system whereby new tires were placed on the drive axles of the tractors and the partially worn tires were put on trailers. However, about 1960, premium cross-lug tires were chosen for the drive axles, and switching has been cut down. In fact, the company has had to buy some trailer tires because the supply from the drive axles has not met demand.

In the trucking industry it is not uncommon for the tire expert to be on loan from a major rubber company. Yellow Transit has had the services of G. B. Grafmiller from the Goodyear Tire and Rubber Company. Cooperation between the companies has been exceptionally workable through the years, and Yellow Transit has provided a proving ground for Goodyear. This affiliation should not lead to the conclusion that Goodyear tires have been used exclusively. Careful purchasing of several brands often resulted in cost savings to Yellow Transit, and in addition, several rubber companies were substantial users of Yellow Transit service.

The real benefit of the Yellow Transit all-new tire program was in labor savings. Tires for the entire fleet were maintained by about five people. Inspectors, switchers, and the like were no longer necessary. In the tire area, also, Yellow Transit substituted capital for labor.

TERMINALS

The second large division of the physical plant of a truckline consists of terminals. The previous management of Yellow Transit had sought to increase the number of terminals through leasing rather than building, a practice that allowed them to expand without investing capital. Some of the leases had been signed with one of the subsidiary terminal companies. Monthly rentals, it was apparently concluded, could be paid out of future operating receipts. Leased terminals are listed in Table 8. The fact that several leases were signed in 1951 was by no means an acci-

TABLE 8
Terminals Leased, 1948-52

Location	Duration in Years	Date
Muskogee, Okla.	5	2/15/48
Dallas, Tex.	20	4/ 1/48
Wichita, Kan.	5	3/29/49
Springfield, Mo.	3	3/ 1/50
Indianapolis, Ind.	3	7/ 1/50
Evansville, Ind.	5	8/ 1/50
Oklahoma City, Okla.	20	9/ 1/51
Amarillo, Tex.	20	10/11/51
Louisville, Ky.	20	10/11/51
Vincennes, Ind.	20	10/11/51
San Antonio, Tex.	3	10/24/51
St. Louis, Mo.	20	11/ 1/51
Ardmore, Okla.	20	11/23/51
Baxter Springs, Kan.	20	12/ 1/51
Austin, Tex.	5	12/15/51
Chicago, Ill.	18	1/ 1/52
Kansas City, Mo.	40	1/ 1/52
Houston, Tex.	20	5/ 1/52

dent; funds were scarce at that time, and many company-owned properties were sold for cash with a lease-back option.

The procedure itself was a legitimate business operation, but some of
the desperate moves created unfavorable rental conditions. Some leases
contained no provision for subleasing, and, although the buildings became inadequate and new quarters were required, the rent did not stop.
Buildings in other locations were leased, only to be abandoned because
the changing character of the Yellow Transit operation no longer called
for a terminal at that point. Ardmore, Okla. was an example of this lack
of foresight.

On the other hand, not all the leases proved disadvantageous. Some
of the long-term arrangements resulted in lower rents than would have
been possible at later real estate price levels. Moreover, some of the
property leased for a long period—the Dallas terminal, for example—
was subsequently purchased, improved, and sold—again as conditions
changed.

The new management group inherited all the good and bad terminal
properties. Slowly, a systematic approach to new additions was established, and months of planning went into the construction of larger
terminals. Two of the first new terminals constructed by Yellow Transit
were built in 1954 in Indianapolis and Tulsa. The Indianapolis dock
featured ten doors on each side and contained an office section that included four sleeping rooms for over-the-road drivers away from home.
The Tulsa building had a small office area, plus seventeen doors in
the dock area. Both terminals replaced existing facilities in the two
cities. Business in Evansville, Ind. soon outgrew the terminal facilities
that Yellow Transit leased there, and a replacement was built. Similar
improvements were made in various cities as needed, but it was in
early 1956 that Yellow Transit made terminal history.

Since 1949, Yellow had served Detroit via U.S. Highway 12 from
Chicago. This route followed the old Territorial Road west from Detroit
and the later Michigan Central Railroad. A series of industrial centers
had developed along the old corridor of commerce, including Jackson,
Albion, Marshall, Battle Creek, and Kalamazoo. Yellow Transit was
determined to tap this market. Each of the cities boasted a fair amount
of potential traffic, but not of sufficient quantity to support individual
terminals. As a result, a new concept in pickup and delivery was developed. A large terminal was established at Marshall, the midpoint,
and pickups and deliveries to the other spots were made from there.
Because the freight was assembled there from all nearby points, enough

tonnage could be gathered to ship through-trailers on a regular basis to key cities in the Southwest, such as Dallas, Houston, and Kansas City.

The cost of handling traffic from say Kalamazoo east to Marshall and back was perhaps somewhat higher than would have been the case with direct hauling. Old-timers commented that hauling east to get west would never work. However, the preferred service that resulted from the process of assembling at Marshall attracted high-quality traffic that made the innovation a success. Submaximization at each point brought optimization to the whole group. As the Yellow Transit system expanded, Lansing and, for a while, Grand Rapids were added to the points served from Marshall, an area terminal.

The success of the Marshall operation confirmed management's theories, and similar terminals were built elsewhere. One of the next moves, however, proved to be an unfortunate one. Mattoon, Ill. was the site selected, and service to a total of 179 central Illinois communities was provided. Unfortunately, the character of the traffic available in that area did not provide the volume necessary for the high level of success enjoyed by other area terminals, and the company was saddled with a terminal larger than needed. Part of the enthusiasm for the Mattoon terminal was based on short-haul business, such as from Peoria to Indianapolis; later, company policy was altered to favor long-haul traffic.

On Christmas morning, 1956, the Dallas terminal was destroyed by fire. George Powell, Sr., Bill Riley, and Dave Padgett left their families and flew that day to Dallas to supervise the immediate setup of temporary operations. The dock and thirty trailers were lost, but the office section of the building was saved. Temporary space was soon acquired, and the rebuilding of the terminal was undertaken on the same site at 6909 Harry Hines Boulevard. The new dock was superior to the old and contained space for the loading and unloading of fifty-one trailers, but the unfortunate destruction was a costly and painful way to improve.

As the company grew and additional space was needed, some terminals were enlarged. After Ohio points were added to the Yellow Transit system, Indianapolis took on greater significance; as a result, six new doors were built there in late 1957, making the total twenty-six. Similarly, the terminal at Dearborn, Mich., which had served Detroit for some years, was doubled in size in 1957; the door total was seventy-two.

Not all the terminals added to the system were built or owned by the company. In some locations, where the long-run prospects did not appear promising or where suitable facilities could be found, the company leased. Changing traffic patterns and company policy toward the traffic to be hauled resulted in some closings. For example, the company discontinued terminals at Lawton and Duncan, Okla. Emphasis on long- rather than short-haul traffic altered conditions to the point where these terminals were no longer advantageous.

Terminal growth continued during the 1960's to keep up with the changing character of company operations. The greatly expanded terminal in Dearborn had been necessary when short-haul traffic was an important part of company business. By 1962, however, the large, old building situated on a cramped lot was judged unsatisfactory, and a new, efficient terminal was constructed on a spacious plot on Greenfield Road in Melvindale. The new terminal featured twelve cross-doors and five end-doors. Land and building cost was approximately $200,000.

In early 1963, a new terminal was built at 4500 Irving Boulevard in Dallas on a site allowing for expansion. The terminal, which took advantage of latest building techniques, had seventy-four loading doors. The freight dock was automated with the conveyor system in the floor, eliminating the excessive noise of overhead "drag" systems. Inside, circulation was increased to relieve heat during the summer. The hot air rose and moved out through passages in the roof, and cooler air was drawn in over the dock. The total cost was around $800,000, but Dallas was one of the major break-bulk points on the Yellow Transit system, and a modern, efficient terminal was required.

The other major break-bulk point was St. Louis, where both dock and yard space had been inadequate for some time. A new site was found in an urban renewal section of St. Louis, and the Yellow Redevelopment Corporation was established to handle the transaction with the Redevelopment Commission in St. Louis. Approximately two years were required for the construction of the new terminal. The new facility, which cost approximately $2,752,000, was described as follows:

Yellow Transit Freight Lines, Inc., has moved its St. Louis terminal operations from 3675 Chouteau Avenue to a new 21-acre terminal at 400 Barton Street.

The tract runs from Barton south to Sidney Street and from Seventh Street eastward to Second Street. A segment of Broadway through the tract will be closed, except for easement as a fire lane.

The terminal is one of the largest common carrier truck depots in the Midwest. The terminal building has 102 loading docks equipped with automatic load levelers. Merchandise will be moved about the terminal floor on 500 carts hooked to in-the-floor chain conveyors, and equipped with automatic switching devices.

A separate truck servicing building has 14 fueling bays with underground tanks and servicing lines capable of handling 100 units an hour. There are 10 bays of servicing shops. An average of 350 units a day will be moving in and out of the terminal seven days a week.

The ground is paved with concrete aprons at the loading stations, and the scales, and with blacktop elsewhere. Exception to this will be in the front blocks between Seventh and Broadway, where landscaping will include evergreen screening.

The buildings were designed by Folger-Pearson, Kansas City architects, W. A. Rawlings Co. had the general contract.

In the main building, in addition to the dock and dispatching area, there are a general office, with private areas for department heads; lunch room, lockers, lounges and sanitary facilities for office help; other lockers and sanitary facilities for 400 dock and truck workers in the terminal; and, on a lower floor, a 64-room dormitory, with lounge, snack room, sanitary facilities, that include baths, lockers and storage facilities for highway drivers. Dormitory rooms are linked by a communication system with the dispatcher.

The buildings are of masonry construction. Private and general offices and the dormitory area have gypsum acoustical ceiling, light grey vinyl tiled flooring, and walls generally of light or neutral paint finish. Private offices and some areas of the general offices have some walnut plywood paneling, however, and the walls of the dormitory units are painted in various colors.

Plans are already being drawn for an additional wing of loading docks to be added later.[7]

Vice-president D. D. Padgett and Burl Cotton, director of terminal operations, were the two Yellow Transit officials most directly concerned with the terminal building.

Few terminals the size of the St. Louis complex have been built. However, the investment in fixed assets by trucking concerns has grown to the point where the old notion of highly variable costs for trucklines has become invalid. The growing number of systems with many terminals and large rolling fleets has placed an ever-increasing portion of total costs in the fixed cost category. The investment in terminals cited for Detroit, Dallas, and St. Louis indicates the magnitude of some of these facilities.

Yellow Transit Freight Lines also constructed a general office building at Kansas City. At the time of the company's release from federal

[7]*St. Louis Post-Dispatch*, May 2, 1965, p. 1.

court jurisdiction in late 1952, headquarters were located at 1626 Walnut Street in a Kansas City building leased from the Evans Electric Company, which also occupied part of the two-story building. In 1955, the Evans company moved and sold the building to Yellow Transit. The company soon outgrew even this additional space, and the new building was started in 1959 and was occupied the following year. The new headquarters was located a few miles south of downtown Kansas City at Ninety-second Street and State Line Road, and was the first building to be constructed in an area now featuring office buildings and a large suburban shopping center. The strikingly modern building, cited for excellence in both exterior and interior design, was "completely divorced from the noisy, dusty, agitated atmosphere of the typical truck headquarters."[8] It was symbolic of the new thinking and action at Yellow Transit.

[8]"Yellow Transit: A Transportation Giant in America's Heartland," *GMC Truck News* (September-October, 1962), p. 4.

8 / INCREASING SALES AND IMPROVING SERVICE

Improving the consist by adding "good" tonnage is the goal of any transportation firm, and this was the job that faced the sales and service departments at Yellow Transit at the time of the Powell takeover in 1952. This chapter will trace the sales efforts, pricing considerations, loss and damage emphasis, and expansions attempted in the effort to improve consist and increase profits at Yellow Transit Freight Lines.

IMPROVING TRAFFIC

The traffic handled by Yellow Transit at the time of the Powell management takeover was extremely diverse, and operational patterns were a curious mixture of short and long hauls, with local[1] runs in some sections. The Powell group soon made the policy decision that Yellow Transit would discontinue its short hauls and become a long-haul carrier. One of the first streamlining moves in this direction was the abandonment of the local runs. (The distinction between long and short hauls was somewhat arbitrary. For example, the 200-mile run from Tulsa to Wichita was considered too short, but the runs from

---

[1] In the transport industry the term "local" refers to the type of run in which the truck or train stops for delivery and pickup at every station en route. For example, Ponca City, Okla. and Wellington, Kan. were two of Yellow Transit local stops or "peddle points" between Tulsa and Wichita.

St. Louis to Chicago and from Peoria to Evansville, both between 250 and 300 miles, were approved at that time.)

Several parts of the operating authority were sold—usually the intra-state rights only. For example, the Fort Scott to Wichita rights were sold to the Jones Truck Lines, Inc. Transactions of this nature require Interstate Commerce Commission approval, and, as a result of the necessary hearings and paper work, consummation of sales often was achieved slowly. However, from 1952 to 1954 the average haul increased from 575 to 716 miles—the new efforts were producing results.

Yellow Transit had traditionally been a large less-than-truckload (L.T.L.) carrier, a policy that was continued. The proportions on a tons-carried basis were 60 per cent L.T.L. and 40 per cent truckload (T.L.) in 1952, and 51 per cent and 49 per cent in 1954. On a revenue basis, however, the figures for 1952 were 71 per cent L.T.L. and 29 per cent T.L.; the 1954 figures were 65 per cent and 35 per cent. The higher revenue per ton for L.T.L. traffic was evident, and the greater drop in the percentage figures by tons than by revenue showed improvement in the quality of the L.T.L. traffic.

The solicitation of traffic that met these broad objectives was the direct responsibility of the vice-president-traffic and sales Hugh Coburn and the staff he was collecting. Some good men from the previous management remained and many new men were hired. At the time of the new management's takeover, Yellow Transit was especially vulnerable to losing employees. The Korean War had enlivened the demand for manpower, and trucklines were still reasonably risky employment spots—many lines were small, and the number of failures and combinations was great. Thus, the Yellow Transit sales force became virtually a new group. Company sales letters, area newspapers, and trucking publications were filled with the many appointments to the sales staff throughout the system. At first the appointments were often replacements, but as the company gained strength many additional salesmen were hired. For the most part, seasoned trucking men were hired in the locales where vacancies occurred. This practice allowed Yellow Transit to gain a maximum of experience in a minimum of time.

The sales force was reorganized as the company stabilized and expanded. Originally, the staff was small enough that each terminal sales manager reported directly to Coburn, and in several locations the sales manager was the lone sales representative. Within a few months, however, some of the larger terminals—Oklahoma City, Dallas, and Detroit—had been converted to district sales offices. The district sales manager's responsibility extended beyond the headquarters city: the manager at Dallas had sales development jurisdiction over Dallas, Fort Worth, San Antonio, Houston, and the Texas coastal area; the Detroit manager covered all of eastern Michigan and the Toledo and Cleveland areas of Ohio.

As the district system expanded, the line of authority went from the vice-president-traffic and sales to the district sales manager to local sales people. By early 1955, a major change in the organizational setup was instituted with the creation of two regional vice-presidencies. Don Sable was promoted at Dallas for the southern region, and Mark Robeson was named northern region vice-president. Although personnel changes in the next few years altered the titles of the regional sales managers, the system remained basically the same. Specifically, in May, 1956, Robeson was named assistant to the president with jurisdiction over employee relations, and his former post was made into a regional sales manager position. In January, 1957, another series of executive changes resulted in the southern region's being headed by a regional sales manager.

One of the first sales plans tried by Yellow Transit involved interline shipments. Each terminal sent monthly reports to the general office at Kansas City indicating connecting lines and the tonnage received from them. From these, trends were noted in the flow of traffic received from connections, and action was taken as necessary to maintain the flow. One obvious reason for such emphasis was that many shipments destined for Yellow Transit points and beyond originated in locations not directly served by Yellow Transit. Through cooperation with other carriers, such traffic could move through the Yellow Transit system.

The amount of interline traffic as a percentage of total traffic was substantial in 1952, when 51 per cent of revenue tonnage was estimated to have moved in conjunction with at least one other carrier. The 1954 estimate was that 54 per cent involved interline traffic; the 1956 figure was 50 per cent. With half the traffic of the company involved, attention to interline carriers was indeed warranted.

Throughout this period, the new management worked out through-trailer arrangements with connecting carriers in some locations. In mid-1954 Yellow Transit and Federal Express entered an agreement of mutual solicitation for traffic moving from such Ohio points as Cleveland, Warren, Akron, and Youngstown to Yellow Transit points. Trailer interchange was accomplished at Indianapolis. Enthusiasm was great for the plan, and it generated a good deal of publicity in the industry. The apparent success led to strong "friendship" arrangements with carriers in other sections of the country, and, when specific through-trailer arrangements were not agreed upon, joint solicitation projects were sometimes undertaken. To cover Iowa and Minnesota, arrangements with the Rock Island Motor Transit Company were worked out in October, 1953. Measures to bring about more thorough coverage of Iowa points not served by Rock Island, and the inclusion of Nebraska cities brought results in October, 1954, when an agreement with Union Freightways was reached.

In time, however, such entanglements became burdensome. Joint solicitation tended to pair up the carriers in the eyes of the shippers, and Yellow Transit inherited shipper opinions of its partner. This did not always prove desirable. Moreover, Yellow Transit was not the sole line responsible for the service rendered and could not control other carriers' service. In the event of trouble, the other carrier could always blame Yellow Transit.

Expansion in partner companies also upset the arrangements, and Yellow Transit finally gave up on this promotion technique. The Federal Express arrangement was promptly ended in March, 1956, when Federal purchased operating rights into St. Louis. As will be discussed later, Yellow Transit itself expanded in mid-1957 through the purchase of Michigan Motor Freight Lines, Inc. Many Ohio points and additional Michigan and Indiana cities were added to the system.

The trend away from interchange traffic was clearly pronounced by the end of 1957 when 60 per cent of Yellow Transit's tonnage was originated and delivered on line. By 1960 the figure was up to 70 per cent, and the 1963 figure was 78.5 per cent on-line traffic on a revenue tonnage basis.

The early years under the new management group were marked by experimentation. In order to balance the traffic flow, some insulated trailers, which when equipped with dry ice could be used to haul semiperishables such as candy, cheese, butter, and so on, were purchased for use in the backhaul. Heaters were acquired for use in the winter when the possibility of freezing was a hazard. In both cases, the possible advantages of providing the special service were considered more important than the extra cost. In time, however, experience showed that such extras were not profitable, and Yellow Transit moved in the direction of preferred service for traffic not requiring special protective attention.

Selling its best service offerings became the keystone of the sales effort. The company has aimed consistently toward high rated, regularly moving traffic not encumbered with special needs or other undesirable characteristics. For example, careful watch on loss and damage experience eliminated some potentially unprofitable business. Even a high price for hauling easily damaged goods could not offset frequent damage payments. The accomplishment of this goal required great effort since the bankrupt line had previously been forced to accept any traffic it could get.

In order to regain the confidence of shippers, good service had to be offered. At first, excessive delays plagued the new group, causing the loss of many newly won customers. Service complaints were frequent. Various plans for smoothing out the system were tried. For example, in July, 1953, yellow expediting stickers were sent to each terminal. The sticker was to be placed on the tally sheet attached to the freight bills of L.T.L. freight that had been in a terminal for over twenty-four hours. Such freight was to be moved out first to avoid further delay.

From this approach to the delay problem grew the Yellow Transit expediting system. Shipments requiring special service were red tagged by the forwarding terminal, which informed the central dispatch office in Kansas City of the need for assured delivery. The central dispatchers alerted destination stations when necessary during the shipment's journey. Expediting assured that all possible care would be given important shipment. As a result, Yellow Transit has had an excellent delivery record in the past few years. Well over 75 per cent of all shipments have been delivered as scheduled, and virtually all special promises for service have been honored.

The matter of keeping promises was of special importance to Yellow Transit. Few lines consistently lived up to their published schedules. The sales people at Yellow Transit flatly stated that their schedules were not necessarily superior to those of other lines, but that Yellow Transit kept its promises. At first, when salesmen were anxious to gain traffic by any means, some on-the-spot proclamations of schedule improvements were made. Through the years, however, such practices have been eliminated, and schedules promised shippers have been maintained. Today the consistent delivery of goods has strengthened Yellow Transit's position with its customers.

Several factors contributed to the ability of Yellow Transit to provide this kind of service. The facilities and equipment policies gave the company a minimum road-breakdown record. The terminals themselves were modernized for efficiency and avoidance of delay. The central dispatch office (CDO), located in the general office building at Kansas City, became the real nerve center of the service system.

The development of the CDO at Yellow Transit was not unique in the industry, but the services performed there were unique. All preferred, or "hot," service shipments were red tagged at the CDO and watched carefully during the move. Since this office had control of shipments over the entire system, it could, for example, hold a trailer in one terminal to catch a special shipment bound for the same destination. In other words, the CDO maximized system-wide service, although it sometimes meant submaximizing a particular segment. The CDO also ensured performance by warning terminals in advance to be on the lookout for the arrival of "hot" trailers at a specified time.

At Yellow Transit the relative autonomy of the salesmen in the field contributed significantly to the success of the sales program. Through the years Yellow Transit salesmen were given more latitude of operation than existed in many other companies where headquarters personnel made frequent and regular field sales calls. Often such visits eroded the shippers' confidence in the local personnel. At Yellow Transit, the goals, quotas, and budgets were established at the general office, but the men in the field were responsible for dealing with the shippers. Consequently, the local salesman came to be regarded by the shipper as the decision maker. The only exceptions to this method were cases of centralized traffic offices in large national firms where a local person was unaware of the total picture and in firms where unique sales conditions existed. In these cases, headquarters personnel made calls; the value of these visits, however, was questioned.

Naturally, the general officers had to have great confidence in the men in the field for such a system to work. Although Yellow Transit people since the Powell takeover have always been reasonably free to perform on their own. quotas and budget checks have evolved slowly. During the first few years. weekly sales letters and frequent sales directives were sent out. These messages often contained procedural announcements. For example, the Kansas City office might watch the loadings by terminals and, in the effort to balance traffic, suggest that everyone particularly solicit, say, inbound L.T.L. to Houston and outbound T.L. from Amarillo. Traffic control tended to emanate from Kansas City by virtue of the experience of the people at the general office. Lists of terminals were published each month in descending order of revenues. Comments were included concerning the successes of certain terminals.

while maintaining a general tone of friendly competition among terminals.

Praise for particular individuals and offices was given when warranted. These comments helped to create a company team feeling while fostering competition among terminals. The traffic potential among the terminals was so varied, however, that some were always on top or on bottom. The personnel at the underdog terminals were bound to be discouraged by the comparisons. The competitive tactics were, therefore, eventually abandoned. Moreover, improvements in the techniques of quota prediction helped the company move away from straight revenue listing. Success in achieving the predetermined sales quota while staying within the prescribed budget became the criterion for judging performance.

The quotas for each terminal were developed by the headquarters sales staff at Kansas City. Field salesmen selected companies in their area with traffic potential for Yellow Transit and determined the dollar worth to Yellow Transit per month. An important consideration for the salesmen was to ensure that only those firms that had shipments of the type desired or potential for such traffic were included. The Kansas City office then checked over the lists submitted and made changes according to the over-all company sales objectives. From these accounts, then, sales quotas were determined. One important function of the general office was to assure the application of consistent standards in selecting potential accounts. The program was successful for Yellow Transit because of two contributing factors—the relatively high percentage of revenues, some 35-45 per cent, which came from the top accounts, and the impressively low turnover of customers. The paper work would be staggering if frequent mass changes occurred. The fact that Yellow Transit customers were steady and satisfied suggested the company had been careful in serving their shipping needs.

In 1957 a reversal of the sales emphasis occurred in conjunction with the acquisition of the Michigan Motor Freight Lines, which added several new terminals to the system in Michigan, Ohio, and Indiana:

During the time we were developing these terminals we began concentrating on the short haul business rather than the long haul traffic that we had been emphasizing during the previous 5 years. Our reasons for making this decision were twofold. First, most of the new general freight business that we acquired from Michigan Motor was short haul in nature. Second, and most important, our management and Board of Directors, as well as many others in the industry, had become quite concerned over the possibility that competition from railroad piggybacking would make inroads on our long haul business. It was felt that development of short haul business could be a hedge against such competition. Emphasis of the short haul business was not only directed toward the newly acquired territory but became our objective throughout the entire system.

We were successful in increasing the volume of short haul traffic during this period 1957 through 1960. In spite of our success at gaining a share of the short haul business, one fact became increasingly apparent. Our earnings were declining in direct proportion to the increase in short haul business. . . .

By the end of the year 1960 we had decided to reverse our policy towards short haul traffic and shifted the sales and operating emphasis to the long haul traffic. We were convinced that we could be of maximum service to our customers, could compete satisfactorily with any form of transportation, and enjoy the happy coincidence of substantially increased profits.[2]

Because operations since 1960 have confirmed this decision, Yellow Transit has continued to be oriented toward long-haul trucking.

TRAFFIC FUNCTIONS

In the transportation industry, "traffic" traditionally has implied both sales and service and the establishment of rates and charges. At Yellow Transit, the traffic department under the new management has been responsible only for the establishment of rates. This function, however, is closely allied to the sales effort of the company, for not even an outstanding sales force can sell fine service at excessive prices. The "rate men," for their part, have been hindered by a lack of information on transport costs—at least in terms of cost units paralleling sales units —and regulation that causes a relative lack of flexibility to change established prices. The result has been that rate men have developed a conservative and protective outlook, while appearing to the outsider to deal in some sort of wizardry in establishing prices.

Thousands of pages have been devoted to discussing the inadequacies of transport pricing. Economists concerned with the allocation of resources into transportation facilities in general and between modes of

[2]Address by George E. Powell, Jr., president, Yellow Transit Freight Lines, Inc., before the New York Society of Security Analysts, Oct. 22, 1962.

carriage within the industry have sought meaningful methods of deriving cost figures for some transport output unit that could also serve as a sales unit.

. . . an optimum transport system requires that rates be based upon costs. Rates are, of course, the prices paid for the 'final' product and must be construed in terms of sales unit. If rates are to reflect costs, it becomes clear that whether transport equipment is geared to the ton-mile or not, a costing technique running in terms of the final product is essential. Otherwise, we revert to a form of pricing on some noncost criterion that, especially where intercarrier competition is concerned, is not only untenable but with freedom of shipper choice leads to resource misallocation.[3]

Unfortunately, no real agreement exists among transport economists on the proper sales-output unit to be used in costing. Moreover, the cost characteristics of transportation service present other unresolved problems. The proportion of fixed costs in some short-run period has traditionally been considered high in transportation. In addition, many goods are hauled at the same time, which results in common costs. A workable method for assigning such costs has yet to be devised.

The essential point is that truckline rate men do not have the tools for pricing on some cost basis, which are available to price setters in most other business endeavors. Therefore, the form of pricing has been based on the noncost criterion of the value of the service. The result has been the misallocation of resources feared by the economist. The rate man at any one company is not as concerned with the over-all economy as he is with the price-cost relationship of his particular firm. That the prices (rates) he sets for his company prove profitable is quite enough of a challenge.

The head of the traffic department since before the Powell takeover was L. E. Tomlinson, a veteran Yellow Transit official. During the years he was in charge of pricing, many refinements in procedures occurred, but, in general, the company continued to aim for the highest rated traffic possible. This plan gave the company the reputation of a "high rate" carrier. Yellow Transit never "sold" rates but, instead, sold superior service at rates commensurate with the service.

[3]George W. Wilson, *Essays on Some Unsettled Questions in the Economics of Transportation* (Bloomington, Ind.: School of Business, Division of Research, 1962), p. 19.

The primary geographical areas of Yellow Transit operation have been a factor in the maintenance of a sound rate structure. Those truck-lines that are members of a motor carrier rate bureau, rather than the independent carriers, have tended to establish the rate structure in the Yellow Transit area. Although some areas have been plagued by the independents, who frequently are rate cutters, companies in the Yellow Transit territory have considered the common goal of all the truckers. Moreover, the rate bureaus themselves have been responsive to the needs of the trucklines and, as a result, have been strong. Sometimes, of course, a company feels that independent action is required. For example, Yellow Transit has acted independently on occasion when a touchy situation seemed to demand setting a poor rate. By setting a rate in-dependently no precedent is established.

The underlying philosophy of the rate department at Yellow Transit has revolved around the difficult concept of the value of service. Since 1952, several factors have been included in the idea of value of service. *First,* rail competition rates were used only as a base because the company maintained that its more flexible service was aimed primarily at small lot shipments, which were not particularly competitive with the mass transportation feature of the railroads. *Second,* shipper needs were considered in a competitive light. Too high a rate might keep traffic from moving at all and could encourage private carriage if the many other variables such as regularity and volume were suitable. Trucker-shipper discussions, according to Tomlinson, often resulted in a compromise, which he called a "sounding rate."

A *third* consideration in rate setting at Yellow Transit was the direc-tion of the movement and the locations involved. The company has had an unbalanced traffic flow toward the Southwest. In other words, the flow of tonnage from Michigan, Ohio, Indiana, and Illinois to Texas, Oklahoma, and beyond was greater (forward haul) than the reverse flow (backhaul). The forward haul became known as the "revenue" haul. This designation came about partially because rates established for the forward haul tended to be higher than rates for the backhaul. Differences in rates for hauling goods in opposite directions over the same routes were based more on competitive conditions than on strict cost considerations.

Operating costs were a *fourth* important part of the determination of rates by the traffic department. Each year the costs of operation (as determined by ICC formula Highway Form B) were calculated by Yellow Transit for the general freight portion of the business and for the total operation including the special hauling division, which primarily carried steel products in the Illinois, Indiana, Ohio, and Michigan region. Highway Form B costs were used as evidence in the many hearings necessary in establishing rates. For company decision-making purposes Yellow Transit used its own cost data.

After the Powell takeover, internal cost techniques were assigned to the treasurer's office, headed by Harold E. Edwards. Various methods for determining meaningful cost figures were tried. At one point revenues and costs per hundredweight were thought to be good measures. Later, figures per mile were tried. Throughout the period, Edwards was concerned with trying to devise some cost figures that could be issued in units similar to sales units. In January, 1961, Yellow Transit became the first truckline to develop a cost by shipment figured on a monthly basis. Before this plan no really systematic costing existed. Basically, the plan was a separation of terminal costs from total costs. Then line haul and other costs were divided arbitrarily and assigned to terminals depending upon their location. Differences in terminal procedures were considered, and particular credits and charges were assigned to unique conditions. For example, Indianapolis was a through-traffic spot and St. Louis a break-bulk location. The totals thus derived were divided by shipments to get a cost-per-shipment figure. Edwards claimed the methods were not particularly scientific, but were based on experience. He also noted that the shipments at Yellow Transit rather frequently weighed the average of all shipments—the mean weight was close to the modal weight. This was an original approach, with the useful feature of easy comparison between costs and rates for a particular movement.

In the continuing search for information about the tonnage handled, the traffic department made a yearly check of the truckload traffic on a sample of shipments during one month from each forwarding terminal. The survey was to determine the amount of traffic moved on class rates as opposed to the portion moved on commodity rates. Since class rates generally are higher than commodity rates, the class-rated traffic was the preferred. In the 1962 check taken during February, 74 per cent of the shipments, 63 per cent of the weight, and 74 per cent of the revenue were accounted for by class-rated traffic on the forward haul. The backhaul showed quite a different pattern—26 per cent of shipments, 17 per cent of the weight, and 26 per cent of the revenue were derived from class-rated traffic. In the backhaul direction, 7 per cent of the shipments, 8 per cent of the weight, and 3 per cent of the revenue were made up of exempt commodity shipments. In both directions the balances, of course, consisted of commodity-rated traffic.

The work of the traffic department was often frustrating. The sales department might have felt certain that a small rate reduction would double some particular movement, but the traffic department balked. Although such stands naturally were unpopular, they were necessary. The rate structures that the company developed in the industry were extraordinarily complex, involving vast arrays of interrelationships and crossrelationships. The good rate man was well aware of the intricacies and was hesitant to disturb one element that might shake the whole structure. At Yellow Transit, unreasonable extremes were avoided, and a measure of desirable caution was implemented. Yellow Transit's traffic department was responsive to changing conditions, yet careful in action.

CLAIMS PREVENTION

The job of the claims prevention man in a truckline is a difficult one. Successful handling of goods involves the entire shipping operation. The attitudes of the employees are an integral part of successful transactions, and the claims man must know how to get top performance from the men and the machines. Safety is also a factor, for accidents on the road or dock can cause damage to the goods. Finally, the claims man must be concerned with proper packaging.

Most of the problems surrounding claims prevention are solved with care on the part of employees. This is a function of a smooth-running, well-organized operation. When the new management took over Yellow Transit in 1952, they found that the truckline's problems were compounded by a high claims ratio. Moreover, since the claims could be postponed, the troubled company had let them pile up. Employees were occupied with just keeping things going. The net result was high cost to the company for lost and damaged goods. In 1952, the costs of claims payments, insurance, and the safety program amounted to about 8 per cent of gross revenues. Not only were these costs a direct drain on profits, but also customer dissatisfaction was great. Losses and damage only delayed the delivery and use of the needed items. For shippers, who often considered the promptness of claims payments when selecting a carrier, the best possible evidence a truckline can present is a record of no claims.

Because costs were high and customer satisfaction low, the new Yellow Transit management embarked on a claims prevention program in 1953. The interest of top management was impressed upon the terminal managers, who were directly charged with improving the conditions that had bred the claims problem. Coding manuals were issued that clearly indicated the proper markings for the various break-bulk stations and destination terminals. Drivers and dock personnel were informed of the necessity for putting freight in the correct trailers. These measures reduced the problem of lost freight. Proper stacking of freight in the trailers and updated transfer techniques within the terminals were instituted to avoid damage. Thus the company was able to reduce the claims problem.

In the industry this area is known as OS&D—overages, shortages, and damages. Os&D clerks are always trying to match "over" freight with "short" freight. At Yellow Transit the communication system between terminals has been a valuable aid. Moreover, the CDO has performed admirable sleuthing service in locating lost items. The company has operated its OS&D section under the concept that freight belongs to the consignee. Salvage has been at a minimum because Yellow Transit has tried to have the consignee accept the shipment with a settlement or to have the shipper repair the damaged items with subsequent reshipment to the consignee. Prompt attention to all claims filed has resulted in the settlement of 90 per cent of all claims within thirty days.

The joint shipper-trucker interest in packaging derives from the common goals of maximizing protection while minimizing weight. In addition, shippers naturally have a keen interest in costs. Yellow Transit often has acted as a consultant for specific needs to packaging companies devoted to the search for new and better methods. Truckline experience in the loss and damage area has been valuable in creating new approaches to packaging and wrapping. Occasionally, Yellow Transit has actually solved shipper packaging problems. For example, heavy transformers were moving in volume and with regularity from a Michigan terminal to points in the Southwest. Since stacking one transformer on top of another was unworkable, portable "shelves," which allowed more than one layer to be loaded, were designed for the trailers. Such efforts have won friends and customers for Yellow Transit.

In 1956 the company began a vigorous safety program. This plan not only protected life and property but also ensured the damage-free delivery of goods. A careful program was written containing specific instructions on how to avoid accidents and procedures to follow in case of trouble. In 1959 a revision was issued, and, since that time, the safety program has been modernized to suit changing conditions.

The whole area of safety and claims prevention involves many commonsense procedures. One very routine but highly significant factor in the prevention of loss and damage at Yellow Transit was the emphasis on housekeeping. Constant effort was exerted to keep terminal docks clean; it was felt that a clear dock would be free of "over" freight and, in addition, would be relatively safe from hazard.

The results of the claims prevention and safety efforts were highly satisfactory. Placing the responsibility at the terminal level created a special awareness of the need for care. By 1960 claims payments were down to below 1 per cent of gross revenues, and the entire insurance, safety, and claims costs were near 3 per cent—quite a reduction from the 8 per cent of 1952.

The success of the safety and claims prevention program encouraged Yellow Transit to take a bold move on Sept. 11, 1960. On that day the company became self-insured (except in Texas where state law prohibited self-insurance). Reserves for all needs were maintained by the company, based on their own experience. One prime consideration behind the move was cost reduction, and results have confirmed the decision. Of course, circumstances at Yellow Transit were unique, and no set pattern of insurance planning for all trucklines can be drawn from Yellow Transit's experience. The low accident rate, coupled with care in handling on the part of the employees, led to conditions under which Yellow Transit could safely and profitably self-insure. By this move the company exhibited great confidence in its employees. Only with the complete assurance that the personnel would continue to exercise every caution was the truckline able to assume the risk function that self-insurance brought to Yellow Transit.

The emphasis on safety at Yellow Transit has brought many honors to the company. A trophy corner, proudly stocked with numerous local, state, and national awards presented to Yellow Transit, was started. In addition, individual drivers have been credited with heroic deeds and have received driver-of-the-month, or year, awards in all locations of the system. Perhaps the finest tribute to the company and its employees came in 1963 when one of its members was selected the top driver of the year:

William C. Nunley was named National Driver-of-the-Year in Washington, D.C. on June 15 as the trucking industry's model of safety and courtesy and occasional heroism. Mr. Nunley is a resident of Baxter Springs, Kansas, and drives a tractor-trailer combination on a turnaround run into Oklahoma and

Texas. His outstanding career spans 30 years and 2,225,000 miles without an accident. During his 26 years with Yellow Transit and the four previous years with two other Oklahoma-based companies, he has never committed a moving violation, nor has he ever been arrested for a traffic offense. Mr. Nunley was the nominee of the Associated Motor Carriers of Oklahoma, Inc., which hailed him as its 1962 Driver-of-the-Year and two previous occasions, Driver-of-the-Month.[4]

EXPANSION, 1952-60

During the first eight years of the operation of Yellow Transit by the current management, expansions were few. The first added route mileage was of modest proportion. On Oct. 1, 1956, Yellow Transit took over operation of the routes of the Hall Brothers Truck Line under temporary authority. The points added to the Yellow Transit system were the Kansas towns of De Soto, Eudora, Grantville, Lawrence, Midland, Newman, Perry, Sunflower Ordnance Plant, Tonganoxie, Topeka, and Zarah. Lawrence and Topeka are the two major cities now served. On Jan. 3, 1957, the ICC approved the merger and Hall Brothers became part of Yellow Transit.

The major expansion of the period was submitted to the ICC on Dec. 26, 1956 and was decided in favor of Yellow Transit on June 10, 1957. Michigan Motor Freight Lines, Inc. of Dearborn was acquired and merged into Yellow Transit in late July, 1957.

Michigan Motor had been in the transportation business since the 1890's, much earlier than Yellow Transit. The founder and president of Michigan Motor, William J. Seitz, had a long career in transportation, which involved both hauling and the manufacture of trucks. His career began in the 1890's with the hauling of wagonloads of lime into Detroit. Poor roads and heavy loads made the trip difficult. Seitz tried to aid the horses by putting a gasoline motor on his wagon, but the horses had to run faster than before to keep pace with the motor. His next effort was the construction of a truck. He received widespread encouragement and decided to make truck manufacturing his business. But this venture was also unsuccessful. Making each of the many parts by hand was time-consuming and costly, and sales were small in volume and were made at low prices.

[4]"Yellow Transit Newsletter," July-August, 1963, p. 1.

In 1911, Seitz returned to transport. He formed the Motor Vehicle Transportation Company and began building a short-haul trucking business. The first order, from the Detroit Metal and Steel Company, required hauling a load of steel to Pontiac—some 25 miles northwest of Detroit. Although delivery took a full day, the service was still superior to that offered by other forms of transportation. Motor Vehicle had proved its worth to its first customer.

In 1918 Seitz bought into a company incorporated on Jan. 9, 1917, which became Michigan Motor Freight Lines, Inc. Originally, the new concern was to be a complementary operation to Motor Vehicle—one a cartage company, the other a long-haul company. Soon, however, the long-haul side of the business became the primary concern. A major factor in this new emphasis was the extensive highway building program in Michigan; in 1919 alone, some 4,500 miles of road were paved. By 1920, Michigan Motor Freight Lines served Detroit, Lansing, Port Huron, Adrian, Monroe, and intermediate points. In 1922, the 275-mile run to Chicago became part of the system. During the next several years, the company's operating authority was extended into Michigan, Ohio, Indiana, Illinois, and Kentucky. The company made the decision early to grow intensively rather than extensively, and almost every major highway in the region bounded by Port Huron, Youngstown, Cincinnati, and Chicago became part of the system.

William J. Seitz remained active in company management until his death in 1947. His sons, daughter, and brother took over the management of Michigan Motor Freight Lines and continued Seitz's policy of close customer cooperation. Hauling steel became the major portion of the company's business, and, by 1955, revenues were over $10 million.

In 1955, Yellow Transit and Michigan Motor were close to the same size in terms of revenue, and total mileage for each of the two carriers was about 19 million. By these standards, Yellow Transit was about to double itself in one move. Geographically, the merger was propitious in adding new Indiana and Michigan points to its system plus putting Yellow Transit into Ohio for the first time. Virtually every major city in Ohio—including Cleveland, Cincinnati, Columbus, Toledo, Dayton, Akron, Canton, Youngstown, and Warren—became a direct service city on the route. In addition, route duplication, especially between Detroit and Chicago, provided opportunities for consolidation economies.

In its report of June 10, 1957, the ICC included the following:

Yellow Transit is of the opinion that had the control and merger been in effect during the entire year, its net income, after provision for income taxes, would have been increased by $450,761, which, if realized, would permit it to recoup the amount paid for intangibles in less than 2 years. It assumes (1) it would retain Michigan Motor's operating revenues of $9,251,344 for 1956; (2) that it would be able to apply to Michigan Motor's operations its own actual operating ratio of 87.8 in 1956; and (3) that it would achieve various economies aggregating $939,085 yearly. Of these economies there would be chiefly (1) consolidation of office and terminal facilities at Detroit and Marshall, Mich., Chicago, and Indianapolis, $41,350; (2) elimination of the salaries of Michigan Motor's executives for whom replacements are unnecessary, $69,650; (3) reduced expense for salaries and wages for general office personnel by the consolidation of work and elimination of duplicate supervision, $175,550; and (4) lower line-haul and fuel costs by increasing line-haul mileage and the use factor of vehicles, by installing high-cube trailers and converting from gasoline to diesel powered equipment, $294,410.

Notwithstanding Yellow Transit's impressive achievements in transforming a debit balance in surplus of $908,841 as of December 31, 1952, to a credit balance of $1,987,204 as of December 31, 1956, and in increasing steadily its gross operating revenues from $7,482,728, in 1952, to $12,394,115 in 1956, its estimates of economies resulting from the unification are optimistic, but based on all the factors present there are reasons for believing that such savings will be substantial and the purchase price proposed to be paid herein is not unreasonable.[5]

Perhaps some estimates were overly optimistic and not readily achievable, but the difficulty encountered was more in the differences of operation between the two carriers than in application of Yellow Transit procedures to Michigan Motor. First, Michigan Motor had been built up by intensive coverage of a small area. Average length of haul in the 1953-55 period had been 223 miles. Second, a large portion of the Michigan Motor business had been hauling steel and steel products on a regular route but nonscheduled basis. Yellow Transit, on the other hand, had averaged close to 700 miles per haul on an extensive route from Michigan to Texas, and its freight was not dominated by any one product group.

---

[5]Interstate Commerce Commission, "Yellow Transit Freight Lines, Inc.—Control and Merger—Michigan Motor Freight Lines, Inc.," *Reports, Motor Carrier Cases*, LXX (Washington, D.C.: U.S. Gov't Printing Office), pp. 474-75.

For the first three years after the merger, the management at the enlarged Yellow Transit attempted to retain the characteristics of both of the former operations. The steel traffic was singled out and placed in a special hauling division. Operation of this division, the steel division, was rather completely separated from the general commodities' part of the truckline. Separate terminals for the special hauling division were maintained, and the management was also assigned exclusively to special hauling. At one time the head of the steel division was the executive vice-president of Yellow Transit, but the special hauling terminals were later placed under the supervision of the director of terminal operations for the entire company. The growth of this division has been steady, but it has been far more modest than the growth of the company in total. It has become a less significant portion of the business, and its share of revenues has decreased on a percentage basis.

Notwithstanding its relative loss of importance, the steel division continued to provide steady and substantial revenues for the company. Its operation was quite different from the rest of Yellow Transit; the drivers owned their rigs and contracted to drive for Yellow Transit. Trips were made when the steel shippers had loads and were not scheduled on a regular basis. Although competition from contract and private carriers was intense, Yellow Transit, as a common carrier, enjoyed the advantage of being able to balance its hauls with return loads, sometimes other products such as glass. Finally, the pattern of activity in the steel division varied from that in the general freight business, and the ups and downs tended to offset each other. This condition led to interesting speculation on the possibilities of purchasing equipment for the steel division and then switching tractors back and forth with the seasonal variations.

The short-haul business of Michigan Motor was exploited from the time of the merger until late 1960, and the policy was extended throughout the system. The mixture of short and long hauls was successful when measured by total revenues but was a failure from the more important consideration of profits. Once again, the short-haul business was dropped by Yellow Transit, and the intrastate rights of the former Michigan Motor Freight Lines were sold. The two companies with widely differing operating patterns had been transformed into a larger system featuring the characteristics of the more successful Yellow Transit. Perhaps the most far-reaching benefits were the lessons in takeover policies learned by the managerial personnel at Yellow Transit.

Not all of the expansion moves undertaken by Yellow Transit were successful. For several years management had been convinced of the need for movement of trailers between the United States and Mexico through Laredo, Tex. and Nuevo Laredo, Mexico. An early attempt was denied in 1956 when the ICC prohibited the purchase of certain operating rights of the Inland Motor Freight Lines. The reasons given were duplication of service and the dormancy of the rights.[6]

Yellow Transit then sought original authority for rights to haul general commodities in interstate and foreign commerce along U.S. Highway 81 from San Antonio to the Mexican border at Laredo. This application was denied Sept. 8, 1960. Next Yellow Transit tried to acquire authority for the international traffic only. This plan was also unsuccessful. Naturally, the profit motive was the impetus for the continued efforts, but great shipper interest was responsible for Yellow Transit's predictions for a successful operation.

Essentially, shippers were anxious for Yellow Transit to inaugurate a new through-trailer service designed to eliminate the delay, expense, loss, and damage that existed after a shipment reached Laredo.

The following was one explanation of the problem:

1. The shipment is off-loaded upon arrival into the warehouse of the line-haul motor carrier.

2. The customs broker to which the shipment is assigned is notified, usually by mail, of the arrival of the shipment.

3. Upon request of the customs broker, the shipment is reloaded into a delivery vehicle for transportation to the warehouse of the customs broker in Laredo, Texas.

4. The shipment is off-loaded from the delivery vehicle in the warehouse of the customs broker in Laredo, Texas.

5. The shipment is subsequently reloaded into a vehicle of a local cartage operator for movement to and across the international boundary.

6. The shipment is off-loaded in the Mexican Customs House in Nuevo Laredo.

7. After clearance of customs the shipment is reloaded into the vehicle of the line-haul carrier for movement into the interior of Mexico.[7]

The proposed Yellow Transit service would have eliminated each of the above steps through an arrangement whereby the trailer doors

---

[6]*Transport Topics*, June 18, 1956.

[7]Interstate Commerce Commission, Docket No. MC-112713, Sub 81, "Yellow Transit Freight Lines, Inc. Extension—Laredo, Texas," exceptions by applicant to the report and order recommendation by examiner Garland E. Taylor, Feb. 18, 1963, pp. 37-38.

would have been closed and sealed in bond at the international boundary. Customs clearing would then have been accomplished at the interior destination point. Notwithstanding the obvious improvements resulting from such a plan, the ICC refused to grant Yellow Transit the authority to establish the requested service. Their position was that existing carriers provided adequate service and possessed sufficient authority to institute arrangements of the type proposed by Yellow Transit.

This chapter has discussed the changing sales and service efforts and the first expansion projects undertaken by Yellow Transit since the Powell takeover in 1952. Although all of the programs were not successful, they did give the management team valuable experience, making them better able to cope with future decisions facing the company.

9 / MANAGERS WHO
MANAGE

During the first several years of the new management at Yellow Transit, a rather standard truckline organizational setup was followed. Sales and operations were separated up and down the line. Vacancies and additions to the staff were filled by persons of known ability. Generally, Yellow Transit acquired people with both functional experience and knowledge of the territory in which they were to be located. The years from 1952 to 1956 were spent gathering the employee force, which included many people drawn from other trucklines and businesses.

By early 1956 the top management at Yellow Transit recognized the need for team spirit among the personnel. Mark Robeson was selected to develop the employee public relations program, and he soon was elected vice-president-personnel. Basically, the objectives of the early plan were to crystallize the company's way of doing things and to establish foundations for the growth of individuals within the company; creating unity in the diverse personnel became Robeson's task. In addition, an organized personnel plan that could serve the company in the future was desired, and both objectives were undertaken at the same time.

In the quest for unity and identification with Yellow Transit, company picnics, parties, dinners, and the like were held. The primary goal was simply to get fellow workers and their wives acquainted. Some felt that employees might accomplish more work as a result, but in time this concept was abandoned. Satisfactory performance and happiness on the job were not necessarily related to social contact during nonworking hours, and too many encounters could even be detrimental. The fact that company operations were spread over a great geographical area also limited the program. After several months, the social gatherings were discontinued. It would be a mistake to label them a failure, however, for they had accomplished their initial purpose of acquainting the family.

The era of the organization chart at Yellow Transit was 1956-60. Organization charts of the company hierarchy were prepared and distributed whenever warranted so that workers would know the lines of authority and responsibility within the company. At the same time, job descriptions were written to cover each of the many functional areas in the truckline. The qualifications for particular jobs and the expected level of performance were also indicated. Training sessions on company-wide, individual office, and regional bases were conducted with the idea of taking the desires of management to the personnel. At the same time, supervisory people were given the opportunity to meet the workers.

Employee attitude surveys were taken. In mid-1956 and again in August, 1958, questionnaires were sent out to each employee. Questions dealt with job security, chances for advancement, pay adequacy, supervision, working conditions, and so forth. The results of the completed forms, tabulated as a whole and on the basis of job categories, were highly informative to management. Problems in areas of employee satisfaction were disclosed and corrected as required. In simplified terms, Yellow Transit had an organizational setup that followed the textbook almost completely, and, as long as people could be found who fit the job descriptions, the system was workable.

Along with the development of the formal organization came several checks and balances such as employee evaluation sheets and annual reviews of pay scales. The salary review came during June-July to avoid any association with the holiday season at the end of the year. Standardized screening techniques of prospective employees were developed to establish such characteristics as credit standing, honesty, and absence of criminal records. Company employees not covered under union agreements were provided extensive life and health insurance plans. The pension plan for the same group has existed for some twenty-five years; a profit-sharing plan has also been established. The area of fringe benefits has been amply covered. The procedures and techniques developed in the areas of the evaluation and judgment of personnel and benefits available to employees were wisely and skillfully designed and have remained appropriate guides and programs.

The rigid organizational setup became unworkable, however, and was abandoned about the time that the short-haul business was dropped in 1960. Organization charts were no longer printed, and a new concept of company organization evolved. In the first step, the old division between operations and sales was dissolved. At each terminal a manager responsible for both functions was appointed. In most cases one of the two men at the terminal was elevated; at some locations, however, the individuals involved were unable to implement the new flexibility. These people were placed in jobs of narrow scope or were not retained by the company. Top level functions were divided between line haul and terminals. The sales vice-president assumed a staff position. This change led to the departure of some of the top people who had been with the company since 1952. The very fast growth and changing conditions at Yellow Transit had made rigidity a binding force. Those who were unable to sway with the new policies sought positions with other companies.

A fundamental change in organization was behind the new scheme at Yellow Transit. Formerly, the problems had been to find men to fill specific positions; now the plan was to carve up the work load in such a way that the best talents of each individual were used. People, rather than predetermined job descriptions, dictated the work assignments at the top level. Naturally, great flexibility was a necessary part of such an organizational setup. As the people changed, so did the organization. However, top management at Yellow Transit felt that the broader the scope of talent an individual possessed, the smaller the change required in organization when the individual moved about. In addition, native ability was considered of greater significance than specific training.

In keeping with these ideals, the Powells gathered persons with unusual personal strengths and abilities for their management team. For training, each of the top officials spent a period in charge of almost every department. For example, Donald L. McMorris was hired as comptroller, later was in charge of administrative departments such as the law and traffic departments, was financial planner, and became the person to whom the line-haul manager, terminals manager, and sales manager reported. This wide experience in every aspect of the company ideally prepared him for the position of executive vice-president. The result of such training procedures was "a remarkably deep—for the trucking industry—and experienced management team."[1] The top management group at Yellow Transit, then, was a team of able men who had gained rich insight into every aspect of the trucking business through actual experience. Moreover, the varied backgrounds of this group, ranging from banking to equipment sales, indicated that they were executives engaged in trucking—not the traditional truckline set-up of truckers engaged in management.

The functions performed by the top management at Yellow Transit were unique in that they *were* top management functions. Long-range company objectives were determined by the top management, and the policies and guidelines for operations were defined. The financial requirements of the company were carefully analyzed and arranged as needed. The headquarters staff devised monthly sales quotas and operating budgets for each of the terminals. In short, the broad framework of company expectations, the boundaries of actions necessary to achieve the goals, and the physical plant required were all planned and organized by top management. The actual daily implementation of the programs was completely in the hands of the terminal managers. All the necessary power and authority was delegated to the terminal managers, and responsibility for success rested with them, too. This characteristic of the Yellow Transit organization was outstanding: it had managers who managed.

Each terminal manager, in addition to knowing the policies and ideals of the company, was equipped with a monthly sales quota, a monthly budget, and had access to the assistance of the entire headquarters staff when requested. Basically, the terminal manager determined the specifics of daily operation; the amounts spent on entertainment, dock hands, or typewriter ribbons were determined within his budget. From whom he got his business and how were also his responsibilities. The terminal managers headed complete staffs of greatly varied size. For example, Dallas was an extensive operation while nearby Sherman was manned by fewer than five people. Since the changeover from the separation of sales and operations, the duties of the terminal managers have included experience in the several areas of truckline activities. In this respect the new setup produced men with a scope of vision not unlike the top management people themselves.

Certainly one of the benefits derived from the new system was its

---

[1]"Yellow Transit—Trucker in a Hurry," *Business Week* (Aug. 28, 1965), p. 61.

training program feature. Formerly, experience in many areas was gained only by switching from function to function. Later, terminal managers were engaged in all functions at one time. The new organizational structure within the terminals contained steps up the ladder through both the sales and operations sides of the business. The varying sizes of the terminals also created a natural training ground in that managers at small stations could be advanced to large terminals. In all, a more formalized training ground and avenue of advancement within the company existed under the changed organization of Yellow Transit.

The benefits accruing to the company from having a continuing supply of qualified personnel were obvious. From the viewpoint of the personnel at the various terminals, the employment atmosphere was greatly improved. First, the autonomy of the terminals gave a greater sense of worth to the managers; they were out to do their best because they got the credit for their actions. Clearer lines of advancement provided incentive to the workers, who could see what the opportunities were. Finally, the employee relations program of the late 1950's created a spirit of Yellow Transit teamwork, which helped company personnel grasp the significance of the subsequent organizational changes.

An important milestone in employee relations occurred in the early 1960's. Previously, some anxiety had existed among the employees as a result of the program of frequent switching about among top management. At Yellow Transit the line-staff relationship was quite unusual. Staff people were considerably more involved in decisions than in most companies. Nevertheless, some question existed about the effect on company personnel, from top management on down, when switches from line authority to staff positions occurred. The personalities of the people involved and their faith in the Yellow Transit organization helped to remove uneasiness, but thoughts about the long-run effects of the organizational setup remained. However, these side effects were far overshadowed by the great workability of the Yellow Transit setup.

Employee cutbacks, such as the one that occurred in 1960 when short-haul traffic was curtailed, also heightened the feeling of job insecurity. Moreover, the hesitancy of many Michigan Motor Freight Lines personnel to join Yellow Transit made a poor impression on some workers. In short, the newness of the management and their programs of experimentation within the organization had contributed to a sense of uncertainty. At the same time, however, politics and angling for position within the organization never had an appreciable influence. The Powells made it a point to discourage such factors by concentrating on skills and deserved advancement. The stability of organization and continued growth of the company during the last few years have effectively removed the last traces of uncertainty in job security.

The distinction between line and staff at Yellow Transit was unique. Line authority was narrow and direct. The terminal managers reported to the director of terminal operations. He in turn reported to the executive vice-president, who reported to the president. Staff positions comprised the rest of the headquarters functions—for example, accounting, sales, traffic, public relations, safety and insurance, and so on. However, staff people worked as closely with the terminal managers as they did with the president or executive vice-president. Cooperation with the director of terminal operations was pronounced. The organization then consisted of more than forty terminal managers who reported directly to the director of terminal operations and indirectly to each of the staff executives. The director of terminal operations and most of the staff executives reported to the executive vice-president. The setup looked unworkable on paper, but it was developed through trial and error and has been highly successful. It we consider two staff activities and five terminals as examples, a simplified organization chart would appear as shown in Figure 2.

The success of the setup at Yellow Transit was attributed to four major factors. *First,* the goals established were obtainable and the policies, guidelines, quotas, and budgets provided firm boundaries within which terminal managers were given free rein. They were not overly exact and constricting. *Second,* the terminal managers were truly the decision makers of the truckline. *Third,* the terminal managers had superior abilities, and they were able to grasp the full range of activities within their responsibility. *Fourth,* communication channels between the general office and the terminals and among the terminals themselves were extensive, and mutual confidence throughout the organization added to its strength.

Mutual respect and confidence among the personnel at Yellow Transit allowed the company to operate on the clean desk approach to management—Yellow Transit managers and executives did not write to one another excessively and were not bound by such mottos as "Give and accept no verbal orders." Since only the budgets and quotas were established in Kansas City and decisions were being made at the terminals, the need for written communications between terminals and the home office was minimized. Within the general office, group meetings and conversation among officials took the place of endless memoran-

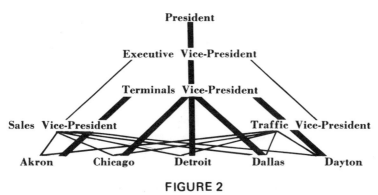

FIGURE 2
Yellow Transit Line-Staff Relationships, Based on Two Activities
and Five Terminals

dums. Wide Area Telephone Service lines provided opportunities for conversation among the terminals; the central dispatch office could connect terminals with one another all over the system. Because the programs were well designed and understood, questions and problems remained at a minimum, and the need for correspondence and telephone conversations was correspondingly low.

Yellow Transit believed that this approach to management resulted in better understanding of problems and their solutions. In addition, real cost savings accrued. Paper, postage, and supplies expenditures were reduced, and the secretarial force was noticeably small. Space devoted to storage of records was minimal. Perhaps the greatest single benefit of the policy was that the people had great faith and trust in one another; no time was wasted securing positions in writing or covering tracks.

Trucking companies have long been known for their stand that the only way to learn the business is through experience in trucking. The Powells' method of recruiting officials to run Yellow Transit was cited by other truckers as an example of how not to gather a management team. Notwithstanding the success of Yellow Transit's top management, additions to the staff through the years have come primarily from other trucklines. The company has sought people who would be productive immediately, and other trucklines have been the training camps. This has meant that such people have not had to be taught trucking, just Yellow Transit trucking.

The organization at Yellow Transit has varied greatly from other trucking companies, and persons trained in rigid companies with definite lines of authority from one man to one boss have found some difficulty in adjusting. As a result, personnel turnover at the supervisory and salesmen level has been somewhat greater than normal, and the company had been rather unsuccessful at injecting people in its higher positions. For one thing, the unique line-staff reporting relationship has contributed to an out-of-the-swim feeling for some; they seem to have failed to catch the spirit of Yellow Transit.

A second area of disappointing performance has been in the training program for recent college graduates. During the first several months of the program, frequent switches from department to department contributed to a feeling of insecurity in the participants. Moreover, the trainees often felt that the tasks they were asked to do were beneath them. Many talented young men fresh from the campus felt they should be making decisions immediately. Difficulties occurred on both sides: the students themselves needed a greater maturity and understanding of the total working mechanism of the business organization; on the other hand, extensive training periods set up by the hiring companies seemed discouragingly more like school than work to many trainees. Certainly one fallacy was the attempt to introduce trainees to every aspect of the business. Not only were the trainees uninterested in several of the functions, but they realized that they would not need even a cursory knowledge of some operations for some time, if ever.

Top management at Yellow Transit has been concerned with the problems of training future managers. They feel strongly that company-trained men possess the qualities that have brought success to the current management group and that they do not have the uneasiness of people brought in from the outside. However, college-trained men often overrate themselves and underrate current employees. Somehow working for noncollege people has lacked status. College graduates have overlooked the wealth of experience and knowledge they could gain from those already in the field. A careful screening process would be required to find those graduates possessing the human qualities necessary plus the technical training desired. New programs would contain bugs that would discourage participants, but in the long run Yellow Transit felt it would benefit from an investment in trainees. Breadth of experience for the trainees would be accomplished by planned moves from sales to operations and the like. In essence, the program of switching top personnel from department to department at Yellow Transit, which gave the current group such rich experience, could provide trainees similar opportunity at a lower level.

THE CORPORATE "PERSON"

Not all the development of Yellow Transit executives has occurred within the company. The Powells were firm believers in contributing talent and time both to related industry projects and committees and to worthy public service programs in general. As a result, Yellow Transit officials in virtually every department have served on many boards, committees, and the like throughout the region and the nation. For example, George Powell, Sr. has been president of the Missouri Bus and Truck Association, a member of the Transportation Council of the U.S. Department of Commerce, and a member of many more organizations. Such associations outside the company have resulted in benefits to Yellow Transit and the industry in general. One prominent example is Mark Robeson's great accomplishment, while president of the Kansas Motor Carriers Association, of achieving the repeal of the twenty-four-year-old ton mile tax.

Most revealing of the character of Yellow Transit is the fact that company leaders have spent a great deal of time helping other working bodies plan improvements and changes. This activity is particularly evident in their dealings with state legislatures and other government agencies. Many state legislatures tend to consider transportation mainly in terms of railroads, not highway shipping. Yellow Transit has tried to reverse this tendency by keeping legislators, highway commissioners, and other officials fully informed of the impact and importance of trucking. The company's philosophy of responsible involvement in problems affecting it also applies to its dealings with union negotiations, rate bureaus, and other organized groups.

In the area of public service, Yellow Transit has been a generous citizen of the community. For example, George Powell, Sr. was a long-time trustee of the University of Kansas City, now the University of Missouri at Kansas City. Robeson was appointed chairman of the Kansas Economic Development Council by Governor William H. Avery to serve for the 1965 fiscal year. George Powell, Jr. has been a trustee of the Kansas City Art Institute.

George Powell, Jr.'s interest in art and association with the Art Institute is especially revealing. He has been a leader in the movement to bring art out of the museums and into lobbies and offices where it is closer to the general public. Under Powell's guidance, Yellow Transit has added to the richness of art collections in Kansas City; a series of water colors by the talented Kansas City artist Frederick James was commissioned, and the beauty and interest of the general office were materially enhanced by them. The tree woodcut that helped Indiana University artist Rudy Pozzatti win a $3,000 prize in national competition was purchased by Yellow Transit before the contest. In the words of the *Kansas City Star,* the Alexander Calder mobile purchased by Yellow Transit is, "without doubt, the finest work of sculpture purchased by a business or organization here in many years. . . ." The *Star* also complimented Yellow Transit on using the right criteria in buying "good" art: " 'Good' in this context means appropriate, original, beautiful, and lasting."

The general office building of the company, completed and occupied in 1960, also demonstrates the concern at Yellow Transit for esthetics. The building, located atop a hill in Kansas City, generates a dignity and beauty seldom found in the headquarters of a trucking firm.

The foregoing examples indicate the major traits of the corporate person at Yellow Transit. From the standpoint of social contribution, Yellow Transit has been a generous citizen. It has also done a great deal to upgrade the image of the trucking industry, which only a few years ago would not have been expected to be a civic or cultural leader.

A second aspect of corporate personality, however, is the often-painted picture of total unconcern for individual employees. This point has two sides: *first,* what top management thinks, and *second,* what the workers feel about the company. Yellow Transit's top management has unquestionably displayed interest in its personnel. Its management philosophy has been geared to the maximum development of supervisory people. It has often been said that "most bosses are far too involved with the day-to-day detail of running their businesses. This is often because they are compulsive workers, and not very good at delegating or at finding the right people to whom to delegate."[2] Yellow Transit's executives, unlike those referred to in the quotation, have indeed delegated and with skill. Yellow Transit has followed the principles described by Ralph Lazarus as management "by influence, by suasion, by example."[3] The basic elements of such a plan are human wisdom and awareness of people. From the company's vantage point, then, Yellow Transit has tried to show every concern for the individual.

[2]Eric Webster, "Let's Repeal Parkinson's Law," *Management Review* (October, 1963), p. 7.

[3]Ralph Lazarus, "The Case of the Oriental Rug," *Michigan Business Review* (November, 1963), p. 4.

What Yellow Transit workers themselves have thought of the company is another issue. Perhaps answers to a few casual questions tossed out at random to workers would shed light on this point. A Yellow Transit driver expressed the feeling that the company was one of the best he could work for, primarily because the leadership was so honest. A dock worker for the company advised a questioner to buy stock now and look the company over later: "The way this outfit runs, it will jump two points by tomorrow." The general feeling among drivers and others who had ample opportunity to observe Yellow Transit employees was that the employees found the company a good one to work for and that they were exceedingly loyal to it.

Employee relations represented a substantial accomplishment, which involved both employee benefit programs and concern for personal comforts. Many companies have these programs but lack the trust and confidence of their workers. The essential difference at Yellow Transit was that management was genuinely concerned about its employees and conveyed that concern in the form of relatively worry-free employment conditions.

Union relations at Yellow Transit also have been amiable. The workers themselves have had the respect of the management, and the company has gone out of its way on numerous occasions to better working conditions without agitation from union sources. For example, Yellow Transit officials believed that the sleeper system, whereby two drivers made a run with one of them driving while the other sleeps, was too demanding on the drivers. All such runs, therefore, were removed from Yellow Transit hauls as conditions permitted.

The general public has often viewed the operations of the Teamsters' Union with alarm and suspicion and has felt that trucklines have had severe problems in dealing with the Teamsters'. While the final center of power within the union has been slowly shifting from the local to the area level and finally to the national scene, the individual truckline has not witnessed a major change in its dealings. The local organizations have remained the primary bargaining units for union-company negotiations. The area and national operations of the union have added to, rather than replaced, the local units. Yellow Transit has worked diligently to establish rapport with the Teamsters' at all three levels. A cooperative spirit has created mutual respect between the union and the company. The company has not adopted a wait-and-see policy but, instead has approached the union in advance with joint issues. For example, before the formalities of hearings in conjunction with the cutback of workers when short-haul traffic was deemphasized in late 1960, Yellow Transit approached the pertinent locals and discussed the problems. Records of operations and the declining profit picture were explained. As a result of this knowledge, the union leaders were cooperative, and the cutback was accomplished with a minimum of difficulty and resistance. In some ways the Teamsters' Union's strength has added stability to the trucking industry. Workers have seldom been on strike and have lived up to their side of contract terms.

The management at Yellow Transit has approached all issues with the philosophy that meeting them directly would produce the best results. This philosophy has brought Yellow Transit into working contact with all types of agencies, ranging from state legislatures to the national Teamsters' Union. Yellow Transit has also contributed conspicuous public service, and while management has been informing others, it has gained insight and knowledge useful for the company. In all of the management's dealings, a more satisfactory climate for company operation has unquestionably resulted.

10 / YELLOW TRANSIT—
ONE CARRIER AMONG MANY

In the span of a few years the trucking industry has grown enormously. The first registrations of trucks in the United States in 1904 indicated some 700 vehicles in operation. In 1939 the number was almost 4.5 million, and by 1963 approximately 13 million trucks were plying the highways of the nation. Equally significant has been the increase in the carrying capacity of all types of trucks. In this chapter some figures on the growth of the trucking industry and its appeal to the investing public are presented; comparisons of performance among Yellow Transit and selected companies have been calculated. Finally, there is a brief look at the transportation market as viewed by the trucker.

TRUCKING GROWTH AND INVESTOR INTEREST

An overwhelming number of trucks are privately owned and are not operated commercially for public shipping. Private owners often haul in direct competition for goods with the commercial carriers. In 1963 some 11.5 million trucks were private, 1.03 million were for hire, and the government owned over 650,000. About 11.8 million were single unit trucks—pickups, dump trucks, and so on. There were 740,000 combination tractor-trailer units, of which 390,000 were private and 350,000 for hire. These combination units may be considered the significant freight hauling vehicles.

Only the for-hire interstate truckers fall under economic regulation by the Interstate Commerce Commission. Within this group in 1963 were some 16,000 trucking companies. For purposes of regulation, carriers are divided into three classes. Class I carriers are those with revenues of $1,000,000 and over per year. In 1962, 1,205 companies were in this group. Class II carriers have revenues of $200,000 to $1,-000,000; in 1962 there were 2,437 of them. Finally, Class III carriers, those with revenues of under $200,000, numbered 13,193. Within Class I, only about 200 companies realize annual revenues above $5,000,000, and Yellow Transit Freight Lines has been one of them. Economic regulation has taken the form of controlling the number of companies and the routes of those companies rather than regulating the number of trucks. Although the latter approach would establish firmer control, it would also make serious inroads into managerial prerogatives, already limited under the existing setup. Carrier health and flexibility may require the opportunity to vary capacity with growth and, in some cases, decline.

Although the number of regulated trucking companies has steadily declined (from over 26,000 in 1939), the revenues of the remaining carriers have grown impressively. In 1939, regulated trucks earned just 17.6 per cent of the total revenue of all regulated freight carriers, and railroads earned 75.3 per cent. The year 1963 was the turning point; trucks had 46.1 per cent of the revenues, and rails, 45.7 per cent. Table 9 presents the yearly figures since 1947.

The trucking industry has made spectacular strides in terms of revenue since World War II. Often such a constant and sustained growth draws the keen eyes and sharp pencils of the investors, but this has not been true of the trucking industry. Many factors are involved in the lack of investor interest. The trucking industry has a record of questionable earnings. Since 1947, the operating ratio (percentage relationship of expenses to gross revenues) for all Class I and Class II carriers has averaged 95.8 per year. Thus, net revenue for the carriers amounts to just 4.2 cents from each sales dollar. Net interest and income taxes are further deductions from the net revenue. The profit margin, in other words, appears slim. However, the capital invested in a truckline can be relatively light, and a line that relies on rented equipment may realize a substantial return on investment even with an apparently unfavorable operating ratio. One problem is that averaging the performances of some 3,500 Class I and II carriers does not provide a reliable measure of any one company.

In addition to the inadequacies of averages resulting from the very wide differences in operating characteristics, information in general has

TABLE 9

Freight Revenue and Percentage Distribution by Regulated Carriers, 1947-64

	Railroads		Motor Carriers		Others		Total
	($000,000,000)	Per Cent of Total	($000,000,000)	Per Cent of Total	($000,000,000)	Per Cent of Total	($000,000,000)
1964	$8.90	45.2	$9.20	46.7	$1.35	8.1	$19.45
1963	8.51	45.7	8.58	46.1	1.51	8.2	18.60
1962	8.34	46.5	8.13	45.3	1.48	8.2	17.95
1961	8.09	47.7	7.46	44.1	1.39	8.2	16.94
1960	8.39	49.4	7.21	42.5	1.39	8.1	16.99
1959	8.68	50.5	7.14	41.6	1.35	7.9	17.17
1958	8.41	53.2	6.13	38.8	1.27	8.0	15.81
1957	9.31	55.5	6.17	36.6	1.30	7.9	16.78
1956	9.32	56.8	5.83	35.5	1.25	7.7	16.40
1955	8.89	57.0	5.54	35.5	1.15	7.5	15.58
1954	8.10	58.4	4.74	34.1	1.05	7.5	13.89
1953	9.31	61.0	4.93	32.3	1.03	6.7	15.27
1952	9.14	62.9	4.42	30.4	.97	6.7	14.53
1951	9.00	63.9	4.17	29.6	.91	6.5	14.08
1950	8.13	64.1	3.74	29.4	.82	6.5	12.69
1949	7.32	67.1	2.91	26.7	.69	6.2	10.92
1948	8.27	71.1	2.70	23.2	.64	5.7	11.63
1947	7.30	73.0	2.21	22.1	.49	4.9	10.00

SOURCE: "Motor Carrier Industry" (Investment research department newsletter; New York: The Bank of New York, July, 1965), p. 11.

been difficult to acquire. Since the late 1930's, carriers have filed annual financial reports with the ICC, but often the information sought by the ICC for regulatory purposes has not been in the form or with the coverage desired by investment analysts. Moreover, the operator-managers of many lines have kept only those records necessary to fill out the ICC reports. In other cases, larger and more sophisticated carriers often have had a number of subsidiaries in nonhauling, but related, fields. For example, terminals and equipment might be owned by a subsidiary and leased to the parent concern. Subsidiary activities do not necessarily appear in ICC reports. In short, the information available is often incomplete, inaccessible, and in an unusable form.

Investment analysts are prone to make intercompany comparisons. Obviously, the dearth of information has hindered this research activity. Vast differences in equipment policies make intercompany reconciliations of questionable accuracy. If consolidated financial statements were available, the problem of subsidiaries would be solved, but the policies of owning versus leasing equipment would still present a problem. In 1945, 21.1 per cent of the equipment of Class I and II carriers was leased; by 1961, the percentage had grown to 39.3. However, the decision to own or to lease is not the point here:

> The growth in recent years of the practice of using long-term leases as a method of financing has created problems of disclosure in financial statements. . . .
>
> It has not been the usual practice for companies renting property to disclose in financial statements either the existence of leases or the annual rentals thereunder. One of the effects of the long-term lease as a substitute for ownership and mortgage borrowing is that neither the asset nor any indebtedness in connection with it is shown on the balance sheet. . . .[3]

With 39.3 per cent of all equipment leased, the precise methods of reporting obviously have an important impact on the reliability of intercompany comparisons based on balance sheet items. The lack of uniformity detracts from the usefulness of such comparisons.

The highly segmented structure of the trucking industry has also been a deterrent to investor interest. The large number of companies and the small size of most of them have contributed to the difficulty of finding outstanding units within the group. In many companies where a former driver has become president, an unsophisticated image and unstable atmosphere have resulted. Many of these managers have had no training even in rudimentary business and financial practices.

Investors have been concerned since wages and fringe benefits approach 60 per cent of gross revenues, and managerial competence in using labor has played a role of magnified importance. A slight increase in labor costs could seriously reduce profits.

The strength of the unions that have organized truck transport workers has been of unusual influence:

> Perhaps more than any other single factor the prominence given the trucking industry's labor situation and teamster union leadership has tended to dissuade investors from providing the industry the kind of market valuation it might otherwise attain. With wage and fringe benefits

---

[1]Cited in John H. Myers, *Reporting of Leases in Financial Statements* (An Accounting Research Study, No. 4; New York: American Institute of Certified Public Accountants, 1962).

costs running about 60¢ out of each revenue dollar, the industry's labor problems are indeed a significant factor in investment considerations. Nevertheless, labor problems should not be overemphasized—in some respects the industry's labor situation is relatively favorable. While threats have been frequent, the industry has actually experienced few strikes. . . .

On February 1, 1964 the new, national three year labor contract that union leadership sought took effect. . . . Most important is the change that occurred within the union structure itself with bargaining and strike calling power now in control of the national authority rather than the union locals.

Few trucking companies expect to find the costs of the new contract which range between 3% and 5% per year, to be any more burdening than previous contracts. While the implications of the power to call a nationwide strike are perhaps frightening to some, it should be remembered that the trucking industry is only the newest arrival on a long list of major industries which are subject to nationwide bargaining.[2]

Limited marketability has been another factor in the lack of popularity of truck shares. The first public offering did not occur until 1939, and by 1956 fewer than ten companies were public. The trend since then toward public sale of common stock has accelerated sharply. Today about fifty companies are public, but fewer than ten are listed. Not surprising is the better performance of the publicly held companies, which tend to be the larger concerns and those with superior management teams.

The initial interest in trucking stocks by the investing public was disastrous, however.

When the drive to consolidate, merge, and simply gobble up smaller companies first started in earnest, many of the big companies got themselves into dreadful trouble. In 1960, for example, Consolidated lost $1.02 a share after earning $1.13 a share the year before, while operating revenues climbed from $88.8 million to $118.8 million. Specter Freight System, Inc. lost 35 cents a share in 1961, and Ryder 11 cents. Other companies remained in the black but only barely. Stocks of the publicly held companies plunged. Consolidated went from a high of 27⅛ in 1959 to a low of 8¼ in 1961; Ryder, from a high of 34¼ in 1960 to a low of 7⅜ in 1962. Many investors were badly burned. The trucking stocks got a bad name, which they have yet to live down.[3]

[2]"Motor Carrier Common Stocks," (Blyth & Co., Inc., 1964), pp. 6-7.
[3]"Here Come the Trucks," *Forbes* (Dec. 1, 1964), p. 25.

Much of the trouble can be attributed to naive and untrained managements that, not unlike many in other industries, regarded increased revenues as the proper measure of business success. These people observed the growing industry revenues, and their own, and concluded that they were healthy. Many explanations of the growth in carriage by truck have been advanced. Flexible, prompt, reliable door-to-door service was unquestionably the number one factor. The decentralization of industry, the construction of many plants in locations without rail service, and changing parts and inventory storage and warehousing procedures have resulted in more frequent shipments in smaller lots with the time factor of utmost importance. Trucks simply were more able to provide in volume and at reasonable rates the efficient service required than were other forms of surface transportation. One widely publicized view has held that trucks have grown at the expense of the railroads. However, gross revenues of the railroads have remained static at the $8-9 billion mark since World War II. More precisely, motor carriers have grown at the expense of railroads in the sense of opportunity forgone; the rails have failed to grow with the economy.

The cost structure of trucklines—the high ratio of expenses to revenues—required a particularly astute management and one with a careful eye for the proper traffic. Gross revenue alone was not the answer. A continuous sales effort directed at profitable traffic, an efficient use of manpower and equipment, and modernization with cost saving benefits were essential to profitable operation. Within the industry few managements possessed the training and knowledge to be called scientific or advanced. Again, significantly, most of the companies that did possess such traits were the large, publicly held motor carriers.

Yellow Transit is an example of a truckline going public. The initial offering of shares was in October, 1959, when 100,000 authorized but unissued shares were issued, and 106,000 shares in the hands of certain shareholders were sold. Blyth & Co., Inc. served as the underwriters' representative in the sale of the 206,000 shares, which received ICC approval on Oct. 12, 1959. The price at which the shares were initially offered to the public was $11 each. As stated in the prospectus of Oct. 21, the purpose of the sale of the shares was to augment working capital and to increase its capital structure. Yellow Transit required additional funds and chose equity financing as the means of attainment.

The timing of the offering was especially interesting. First, since only a small number of companies at that time were publicly held, Yellow

Transit became part of an elite group. Second, Yellow's move came just at the time of the initial interest in trucking stocks—the interest that subsequently stung many investors. Third, Yellow Transit was engaged in its push for revenues by soliciting short-haul business, and its revenues were advancing in the pattern of many carriers. However, unlike many other managements in the industry, Yellow Transit's group noticed declining profits concomitant with the growing revenues. They responded by promptly weeding out the unprofitable traffic, and profits made a fast recovery. This decisive action clearly put Yellow Transit in the class that *Forbes* has dubbed "the new breed." In fact, the entire managerial performance at Yellow Transit since the Powell takeover in 1952 warranted that description.

The motor carrier industry was highly segmented, and the characteristics of units within the group were so widely divergent that generalizations from an operating or investment point of view were questionable at best. At the same time, however, this condition meant that the skilled and thorough investment analyst was given an unusual opportunity. The proper choices could be highly profitable, and for the most part those companies with superior operating records were the companies in which to invest.

COMPANY COMPARISONS

Notwithsanding the acknowledged shortcomings of intercompany comparisons and the extremes that go into industry averages, some operating figures do indicate relative performances. Table 10 presents figures on the general performance of Yellow Transit and a few other publicly held companies.

The operating results shown indicate clearly the effect of the short-haul business at Yellow Transit. Since de-emphasis of short-haul business in late 1960 and early 1961, revenue and earnings gains have been impressive. Perhaps most significant is the steady reduction in the operating ratio. Of the few companies shown, only Transcon Lines has a similar record. Both companies were well below the industry average and have been cited for these achievements: ". . . operating ratios of about 85% are not uncommon . . . Transcon Lines last year had an operating ratio of 84.5%; Yellow Transit Freight Lines, 85.2%. Most of the big lines have an operating ratio of about 95%."[4]

---

[4]"Here Come the Trucks," p. 27.

TABLE 10
Selected Company Comparisons, 1959-64*

(in thousands)

	Operating Revenue	Net Income	Operating Ratio	Earnings/ Share
Yellow Transit				
1964	$42,620	$3,173	84.6	$2.83
1963	35,537	2,515	85.2	2.24
1962	29,745	1,637	88.7	1.46
1961	27,346	716	93.8	0.62
1960	32,013	486	96.3	0.42
1959	31,339	943	92.8	0.83
Associated Truck				
1964	34,090	1,105	93.6	1.64
1963	31,412	808	94.6	1.19
1962	27,006	872	93.8	1.28
1961	23,593	763	95.1	1.10
1960	16,803	431	95.1	0.61
1959	....	....	96.0	....
Denver-Chicago				
1964	50,107	2,562	89.4	2.02
1963	45,709	2,099	90.9	1.64
1962	45,435	1,548	91.8	1.20
1961	46,500	2,036	90.5	1.58
1960	46,467	2,022	90.6	1.58
1959	45,302	1,540	93.3	1.24
Garrett				
1964	36,371	2,153	91.1	2.66
1963	33,769	1,217	92.4	1.50
1962	31,168	1,548	93.6	1.91
1961	19,125	1,251	87.3	1.95
1960	18,234	819	91.7	1.31
1959	....	....	87.9	....
Gateway				
1964	41,511	1,893	91.3	1.88
1963	36,563	804	94.5	0.81
1962	35,563	747	94.7	0.75
1961	31,068	810	93.7	0.88
1960	28,595	375	96.3	0.41
1959	23,785	441	95.6	0.76
Transcon				
1964	32,347	2,522	84.6	3.61
1963	30,295	2,203	84.5	3.15
1962	27,172	1,505	88.0	2.30
1961	24,090	968	90.8	1.52
1960	22,570	382	94.9	0.61
1959	19,347	637	90.0	1.12

*Industry operating ratios averaged 95.1 in 1964, 96.0 in 1963, 95.7 in 1962, 96.0 in 1961, 98.0 in 1960, and 95.7 in 1959.
SOURCE: "Motor Carrier Common Stocks" (Blyth & Co., Inc., 1964-65).

Most of the trucklines in Table 10 have shown marked increases in revenues. Noteworthy, also, is the fact that all the other systems made acquisitions during this period that added to revenues. Yellow Transit grew internally and made no route purchases. Not indicated in the table are the figures of the net income as a percentage of revenues. In 1963 and 1964, the percentages were as follows: Transcon, 7.2 and 7.8; Yellow Transit, 7.1 and 7.4; Garrett, 5.9 and 3.6; Denver-Chicago, 5.1 and 4.6; Gateway, 4.6 and 2.2; and Associated Truck, 3.2 and 2.6. Again Transcon Lines and Yellow Transit led the group and were well above the average of 3.5 per cent for publicly held companies.

Table 11 presents a distribution of the revenue dollar. The three accounts covering equipment (transportation, depreciation, and equipment maintenance) differ widely in the table. The variation results from the particular procedures followed by the companies. A carrier that leases or rents equipment will tend to have a larger transportation cost because "purchased transportation" falls in that account. In the same way, a company that owns its equipment outright will tend to have larger depreciation and equipment maintenance accounts. Combining the three does not provide a meaningful comparison among carriers because the depreciation account, for example, includes fixed property elements such as terminals. Also, the specific arrangements between a truckline and its subsidiaries, which may lease the parent equipment and terminals, negate the validity of comparisons. In one case the parent may pay license, costs, fees, and the like, while in another company the subsidiaries pay. Variations in the operating taxes and licenses account also develop from the specific arrangements. In the taxes-license account the domicile of the truckline can be significant. One state may require a greater proportion of home state licensing than another, and the fees vary from state to state. The elements making up specific accounts and the reporting schemes followed by the carriers are too diversified to allow direct comparisons.

Table 11 does serve a valuable purpose, however. A carrier with a consistently superior performance in any one area appears below the average in expenditures in that account. The table indicates that each company represented possesses some area of special competence. The figures for Yellow Transit are close to or well below average in each expenditure account and well above average in the net revenue account. Such widespread efficiency certainly indicates good management across the board.

Truckline operations analysts often attribute first-class performance to factors such as length of haul, the percentage of total traffic originated

TABLE 11
Distribution of the Revenue Dollar, 1961-63

	Traffic	Equipment Maintenance	Insurance and Safety	Trans-portation	Depreciation	Terminal	Operating Taxes and Licenses	Administrative and General	Net Revenue
Class I carriers									
1963	3.0	9.2	3.8	49.5	4.3	14.3	6.3	5.5	4.1
1962	3.0	9.6	4.0	49.3	4.4	13.8	6.2	5.5	4.2
1961	3.0	9.4	4.0	49.0	5.1	13.8	6.0	5.7	4.0
Yellow Transit									
1963	4.0	8.2	2.8	44.5	0.5	14.8	5.9	3.5	15.8
1962	4.3	8.1	3.2	44.8	0.3	15.5	6.4	4.1	13.3
1961	5.0	9.4	3.3	47.0	0.7	16.8	6.2	4.6	7.0
Associated Truck									
1963	3.1	1.2	3.1	57.4	1.5	22.3	3.8	3.7	3.9
1962	3.4	0.9	3.2	56.8	0.8	22.7	3.4	3.9	4.9
1961	3.3	1.5	3.3	56.6	2.6	21.6	3.7	4.1	3.3
Denver-Chicago									
1963	5.1	13.2	3.2	36.9	4.6	14.7	7.5	5.7	9.1
1962	5.0	14.0	3.5	36.6	5.7	13.8	7.5	5.8	8.1
1961	5.2	15.0	3.7	34.9	4.6	13.6	7.4	6.1	9.5
Garrett									
1963	2.8	10.0	2.9	37.7	5.0	22.0	9.0	4.4	6.2
1962	2.7	11.1	2.8	37.4	4.3	21.4	9.0	4.7	6.6
1961	3.0	10.9	2.7	34.9	5.0	19.2	8.5	4.8	11.0
Gateway									
1963	2.7	10.7	3.8	45.0	3.3	20.1	6.4	3.5	4.5
1962	3.4	11.3	3.6	46.0	2.3	19.1	6.5	3.6	4.2
1961	3.1	11.5	4.0	46.1	1.7	18.8	6.4	3.6	4.8
Transcon									
1963	5.5	9.1	3.6	30.6	4.4	18.5	6.8	5.9	15.6
1962	5.6	9.7	3.9	30.1	4.9	20.1	6.9	5.9	12.9
1961	5.1	11.0	4.8	30.2	5.4	21.2	6.9	6.1	9.3

SOURCE: Class I carrier figures from "Statement Q, Bureau of Transport Economics and Statistics," Interstate Commerce Commission, 1962, 1963; company figures from *Motor Carrier Annual Report Form A* for carriers and years indicated.

and delivered on line, or the proportion of T.L. traffic to L.T.L. traffic. Table 12 indicates some of these figures. The sample is too small to make sweeping generalizations, but the magnitudes themselves are informative. Lack of a consistent pattern within this sample might render questionable the importance of any one factor. All the carriers

TABLE 12
Selected Operating Characteristics, 1961-63

	Number of Truckload Shipments	Number of Less-Than-Truckload Shipments	Per Cent Revenue, Truckload	Per Cent Revenue, Less-Than-Truckload	Average Haul (miles)	Per Cent Traffic on Line
Yellow Transit						
1963	49,760	987,643	43	57	583	79
1962	43,711	907,601	43	57	569	79
1961	39,656	974,693	41	59	535	83
Associated Truck						
1963	58,463	2,177,701	28	72	187	81
1962	51,760	1,953,252	29	71	189	82
1961	42,223	1,790,966	28	72	188	83
Denver-Chicago						
1963	22,697	1,548,028	31	69	1,471	37
1962	23,109	1,525,630	32	68	1,460	36
1961	22,910	1,530,045	32	68	1,459	40
Garrett						
1963	31,775	2,107,103	31	69	544	76
1962	30,121	2,068,563	31	69	506	77
1961	14,927	1,097,283	33	67	681	68
Gateway						
1963	72,687	1,950,687	41	59	316	74
1962	72,644	1,957,034	42	58	312	74
1961	63,134	1,941,129	40	60	320	71
Transcon						
1963	14,545	1,124,677	29	71	1,268	38
1962	13,981	1,127,491	27	73	1,127	38
1961	14,325	1,119,307	26	74	1,101	35

SOURCE: *Motor Carrier Annual Report Form A* to the Interstate Commerce Commission for carriers and years indicated.

derived over 50 per cent of their revenues from L.T.L. traffic, yet the two best performers, Yellow Transit and Transcon Lines, were at the extremes of the range. In length of haul Transcon was at the long end, and Yellow Transit was near the middle. The percentage of traffic on line was greatly different for the two, also.

Since payroll costs were the largest single truckline expenditure, a breakdown by category of the number of people would be informative. Unfortunately, no satisfactory comparative measure of manpower use efficiency exists, for the same reasons that other intercompany comparisons were weak. For example, the truckline that has its maintenance done outside has fewer maintenance employees than the line that does its own work. These shortcomings notwithstanding, Table 13 does contain some significant points. First, the magnitudes themselves indicate the relative number of persons employed by the trucklines. Second, the particular classification is important in terms of cost. Administrative, general, and maintenance and garage employees tend to receive higher salaries than terminal workers, so a balance in favor of terminal employees results in lower total labor costs. Third, a rough idea of efficiency can be gained by the number of employees per revenue figure. Yellow Transit came in about midway in the sample in terms of total employees but showed an impressive downward trend. Also, its small number of administrative and general employees confirmed the limited paper flow policy mentioned in Chapter 9. Yellow Transit did have fewer employees at headquarters than did most other trucklines. Finally, since the wage share of the revenue dollar was the largest portion, the categories of workers closely parallel in relative size the divisions of the revenue dollar. Table 13 presents the distribution of workers by category.

The tables in this chapter confirm the absence of any specific measuring device for intercompany comparisons, which forces the analyst to rely on judgments of management capability. As Blyth & Co., Inc. puts it: "Without question the most important single factor in evaluating the prospects for a motor carrier is the competence and depth of management."[5]

THE TRUCKLINE'S MARKET

Management's ability in a trucking company was also tested by its approach to the complex transportation market. The prognosticator of the aggregate transportation movement and dollar cost was quite able to look at total economy performance statistics and the expectations for the future and predict with accuracy the proportion of GNP that would be accounted for by transport. Wide arrays of facts and figures were available on the total picture; however, the composition of the statistics made the figures meaningless to the individual company. Figures on total industry output were collected and plugged into formulas; predictions were then prepared. The individual company could, of course,

[5]"Motor Carrier Common Stocks."

TABLE 13
Distribution of Workers by Category, 1961-63

	Operating Income ($000,000)	Average Employees per $1 Million Revenues	Average Intercity Power Units	Average Employees per Power Unit	Average Total Employees	Traffic and Sales	Maintenance and Garage	Insurance and Safety	Transportation	Terminal	Administrative and General
Yellow Transit											
1963	$34.1	60	532	3.8	2,061	82	120	11	1,178	617	53
1962	28.7	64	492	3.8	1,872	88	111	12	1,036	574	51
1961	25.8	73	486	3.9	1,883	109	139	13	983	582	57
Associated Truck											
1963	31.3	65	422	4.8	2,025	65	17	18	1,100	754	71
1962	26.9	69	395	4.7	1,849	59	9	16	988	707	70
1961	23.4	71	366	4.6	1,673	53	8	16	917	614	67
Denver-Chicago											
1963	45.1	52	319	7.4	2,364	148	284	33	1,084	709	106
1962	43.9	58	322	7.9	2,552	162	329	34	1,166	747	114
1961	42.2	57	328	7.3	2,394	151	326	32	1,072	695	118
Garrett											
1963	33.7	68	411	5.6	2,289	85	165	12	1,103	796	88
1962	31.1	73	392	5.8	2,268	80	175	16	1,127	773	97
1961	19.1	69	288	4.6	1,314	55	120	8	641	422	58
Gateway											
1963	36.5	72	674	3.9	2,628	72	295	52	1,311	816	83
1962	35.3	74	585	4.4	2,599	74	300	48	1,281	1,000	77
1961	31.0	80	563	4.4	2,477	71	275	42	1,279	713	78
Transcon											
1963	30.3	54	248	6.6	1,650	106	192	8	715	534	95
1962	26.5	59	224	6.9	1,560	110	183	8	660	506	87
1961	23.9	63	226	6.6	1,511	105	176	8	646	430	83

SOURCE: *Motor Carrier Annual Report Form A* to the Interstate Commerce Commission for the carriers and years indicated.

compare its own performance record to that of the industry, and in many cases could come up with accurate and meaningful figures of its own revenue prospects. The composition of its own revenue totals and the shippers from whom the trucker could expect business were hardly disclosed by such big picture calculations, however.

Lack of satisfaction with the aggregate approach led many companies to follow the opposite tactic. Reams of facts were gathered about companies located within the territory served by the trucker. Factors relating to products, their movement and volume were figured as closely as possible; changes of all kinds were watched. Unfortunately, the final data represented isolated bits and pieces and did not provide the whole picture. Moreover, the individual truckline very often had a real problem finding out what it could expect in the way of tonnage from a specific shipper. The competition from other truckers and other modes of transportation encouraged the shipper to be silent. He was thus able to dole out favors in return for favors. In some cases the truckline was able to determine its share of some shipper's business in a particular move by watching the start and destination points; however, few trucking companies could afford the time or the staff for this approach.

The failure of these two methods of culling usable information about the available transportation market created a second test of management acumen and expertise. Not only did the truckline management have to combine the many elements of operating procedure in the proper mix, but the mix also had to be designed to appeal to specific shippers. In other words, the unusually successful truckline had to gear its operations to particular shippers and satisfy their needs consistently. This marketing approach appears obvious, yet countless truckline managements continued to adhere to a policy whereby the trailer was moved only when it was full, be that the next day or the next week.

The skillful truckline management, then, kept informed of the industry pattern and changes in its territory, but concentrated its effort on the small segment it could best serve. Naturally, growing companies destined to continued shipping were the prime targets. The basic lack of knowledge about the whole market was replaced by information about specific parts.

The entry to the market segment any one trucker was best equipped to handle was also a point of great interest. Yellow Transit Freight Lines for several years has held the view that having a reputation for superior service and reliability of promise is the best possible way to attract business. Its advertising program has definitely been of the word-of-mouth variety. Because Yellow Transit has approached its marketing program with the view that traffic managers make the shipping decisions, the advertising dollar has been spent in a manner considered best for appealing to them. Newspaper and trade journal ads have been virtually nonexistent. Individualized gifts—ball point pens, key chains, and note pads—have been used.

In view of the limited scope of Yellow Transit advertising and the small group to which appeals were directed, its approach has been successful. Naturally, other trucklines have had other views and goals in their advertising programs. Some lines have definitely appeared to have placed advertisements with public relations and stockholder appeal in mind. As yet, however, Yellow Transit has not been in that group.

11 / Yellow Freight
System, Incorporated

The transformation of the Yellow Cab Transit Company from an Oklahoma City bus operation, to a truckline, to the Yellow Freight System required more than 40 years of effort. This chapter will relate the decisions of the board of directors that converted the truckline into a diversified freight system. With the consummation of the merger with Watson-Wilson Transportation System, Inc., on Dec. 9, 1968, the corporate name was officially changed to Yellow Freight System, Inc.

YELLOW FORWARDING COMPANY

In the spring of 1960 the board of directors of Yellow Transit Freight Lines, Inc. approved a contract for the purchase of two Illinois-chartered companies, the Central States Freight Service, Inc. and the A & G Transport Company, Inc. Central States was a freight forwarding company with authority to operate in 31 eastern and midcontinent states. The A & G Transport Company was a local cartage company used in conjunction with the freight forwarder operations of Central States. The acquisition was based on three main points. First, for a modest sum (at least when compared to motor carrier authority costs) Yellow Transit was able to pick up geographically extensive operating rights. Second, the purchase of the forwarder was a diversification move within Yellow Transit's general business area. Third, and probably most important, the forwarder was considered a fine insurance policy for combating a piggyback surge. By purchasing Central States, Yellow Transit would not only have stopgap protection against possible piggyback competition but would also be able to join the boon, should it develop.

Initially, Yellow Transit operated Central States, mainly a Chicago to New York forwarder of export traffic, as a separate function. The forwarder used railroad labor and warehousing for its operations in a manner that primarily benefited the railroads. The company's costs were high, volume moderate, and return low. During the two years after acquisition, Yellow Transit changed the character of the forwarder completely. The eastbound export traffic was dropped and replaced by westbound traffic from New York and Boston. The new traffic was transported by piggyback to the Chicago and St. Louis gateways and then into the Yellow Transit system for ultimate delivery by truck. As business grew, additional terminals were opened in the East, notably in Philadelphia and Baltimore. Moreover, service was channeled completely through the St. Louis gateway.

The forwarder operation was gradually integrated into the Yellow Transit system. Terminals in Chicago were vacated, and the forwarder moved to the truck terminals of Yellow Transit. The management functions of the forwarder were also separate from the parent truckline. Originally, a vice-president of Yellow Transit headed the forwarder. The integration process dissolved this separation, and the truckline personnel began to manage and operate the forwarder as part of their regular work.

The changeover was costly, and for several years the forwarder failed to make a profit. With each change, however, service improved, and the volume and quality of traffic went up. In late summer, 1963, the name Central States Freight Service was changed to the Yellow Forwarding Company. The service of the forwarder met the Yellow Transit quality, and the change also facilitated the identity of the coordinated service under the "Yellow Freight System" banner. Although the official corporate name at that time remained Yellow Transit Freight Lines, Inc., in October, 1963, a new identification symbol of the company was designed and put into use. The new mark featured the three words, Yellow Freight System. The coordinated freight system had been developed by adding carefully selected operating rights of the forwarder to the truckline. The result was an ingeniously compatible combination that, in effect, extended Yellow Freight System operations to the eastern seaboard. In the process, the competitive threat of piggybacking, which in the late 1950's looked ominous, was overcome. Virtually no single line rail service existed in the eastern and western areas served by the Yellow Freight System.

The board of directors that authorized the purchase of the forwarder was essentially the same group that had guided Yellow Transit Freight Lines since 1953. During the next few years, following a death, a resignation, and the retirement of 4,900 shares of preferred stock that had grown out of the reorganization of 1952, three changes in the board occurred. In 1962 Dr. L. L. Waters, university professor of transportation and business history of the Graduate School of Business, Indiana University, was elected a director. Professor Waters had previously been associated with George Powell, Sr. on the Transportation Council of the Department of Commerce. Later in 1962 Donald L. McMorris, a vice-president of the company, was elected a director. In 1964 an additional outside director was named. R. L. Wagner, president of the Great Lakes Pipe Line Company, brought experience and knowledge of another mode of transport to the board. The four veteran directors were George E. Powell, Sr., chairman; George E. Powell, Jr., president; Kenneth E. Midgley, partner in Swanson, Midgley, Jones, Eager and Gangwere, Attorneys, and secretary of the company; and L. H. Brickman, owner, L. H. Brickman Company.

From the purchase of the forwarder until early 1965 the board of directors approved no additional acquisitions. The period was marked by substantial internal growth. Earnings per share that had been $0.42 in 1960 jumped to $2.83 per share by 1964. Total revenues in the four-year span grew from $32.0 million to $42.6 million. Improvements were varied and numerous. During 1961 and 1962 the road tractor fleet was replaced, and in 1962 the trailer fleet was renewed. Throughout the 1960-64 period several new terminals were opened. In 1962 Flint, Mich., and Joliet and Rockford, Ill. became new terminal points, and a newly constructed replacement terminal building was opened at Detroit. In 1963 a replacement building opened at Dallas. Four new terminal locations began operation in 1964 at Canton, Sandusky, and Warren, Ohio, and Gary, Ind. All of the new terminals were in locations that had been service points previously served from other terminals. The additional openings brought direct service to the cities added and relieved the mounting space pressures at central locations such as Chicago.

The 1961 decision to emphasize long-haul service, for example, was carried out and brought profitable results. The Yellow Forwarding

Company also continued to grow as terminals were opened on the eastern seaboard, and additional shippers used the forwarding operation for the movement of goods from the Boston-New York-Philadelphia area to the states of Missouri, Kansas, Oklahoma, and Texas. During the first half of the 1960's management concentrated on implementing the several operating procedures, policies, and plans that had been developed over the previous several years. The skill with which the pieces of the puzzle were put together documented the quality of the management team and resulted in the spectacular growth in profits. Yellow Freight System was running smoothly.

By 1964 the board of directors faced a new problem: the company had a surplus of top management. The goal of bringing the company to a high level of managerial efficiency had been met, and operating the firm had become second nature to the executive group—all of whom had been seasoned on the frequent changes and the tough problems faced by the company. At this time in the evolution of Yellow Freight System fresh challenges were needed to prevent the loss of capable men.

During the same period a new external force emerged. At the same time that Yellow Freight System was improving both in geographic coverage and in reliability, the willingness of customers to rely more heavily on a few firms or even on a single transportation firm developed. This trend occurred for several reasons. Shippers can enjoy certain economies of scale by dealing with a few carriers. Paperwork is decreased, and fewer individual shipments of a larger size are tendered. Also, carriers tend to be more accommodating to important shipping customers. Happily, carriers also benefit from the shippers' economies. Equipment utilization can be improved with fewer but larger loadings. Productivity of the sales efforts may be improved through fewer calls on better customers. The point is that both shippers and carriers could profit through the economies of scale that were possible with extensive geographic coverage and intensive service patterns. The possibility that a single carrier could satisfy a particular shipper's needs was obviously improved by carrier size. The implications for Yellow were evident.

WATSON-WILSON TRANSPORTATION SYSTEM, INCORPORATED

On Feb. 2, 1965, the company signed a contract that spelled out a cash and exchange-of-stock plan whereby Yellow Freight System acquired control of the Watson-Wilson Transportation System, Inc. The contract was negotiated with the majority stockholders of Watson-Wilson. On May 26, 1965, Yellow Freight System made the offer available to other stockholders not parties to the Feb. 2 contract. Both of these offers were based on unaudited statements and contained provisions for cancellation in the event that an audit disclosed a difference in net stockholders' equity of more than $350,000. The subsequent audit, which indicated a reduction of over $2 million, was delivered to Yellow Freight System on Sept. 3, 1965. Yellow Freight System decided to exercise its right to cancel its agreement of Feb. 2 with all stockholders except those who desired to continue the agreement with certain modifications. On Sept. 24, 1965, the modified agreement was offered to the Watson-Wilson stockholders. The modification involved the cancellation of a $500,000 contract signed by Watson-Wilson, which Yellow Freight System had previously agreed to assume and called for the retention of ownership and control of Star Forwarders and Globe Freight Service.

The plan called for the exchange of at least two-thirds and up to 100 per cent of the Watson-Wilson stock on the basis that for every 100 shares of Class A Watson-Wilson or 200 shares of Class B Watson-Wilson, Yellow Freight System would issue 15 shares of its stock and pay $175 in cash. Fractional shares of Yellow were not to be issued and were to be settled by cash payment of the corresponding fractional part of $30. Based on that price of $30 for each share of Yellow Freight System stock, the whole transaction amounted to about $11.8 million. The effect of the audit and agreement modification was to increase the figure Yellow Freight System was willing to pay for Watson-Wilson, including Star and Globe, by $1.5 million.

The Watson-Wilson Transportation System, Inc. grew out of the determination and hard work of the three Watson brothers, Ray E., Thomas W., and Fay V. In 1926 the company was established with a run between Auburn and Omaha, Neb. The brothers incorporated as Watson Bros. Transportation Co., Inc. in Nebraska on Jan. 12, 1932, with the brothers as directors of that firm. By 1940 the line operated in Colorado, Illinois, Iowa, Kansas, Missouri, and Nebraska, with the operating authority covering more than 6,300 miles. In 1940 operating revenue totaled $1.8 million, 463 employees had earned $659,084, but, net income was just $6,908. Six shareholders owned 1,076 shares. By 1945 points in Minnestoa had been added to the authority, which totaled 7,777 miles. Operating revenues were $3.8 million; a loss of $168,186 had been sustained that year. The number of shareholders had been reduced to three—the Watson brothers. After World War II the system was extended into New Mexico, Arizona, and California. By 1955 operating revenues had grown to $27.0 million, and net income was $345,401. The three brothers still comprised the entire stockholders' list.

Operation of the Watson Bros. Transportation Co., Inc. was closely guided by Fay Watson, the president, who personally supervised dispatching operations and maintained his office hours during the 8 P.M.-8 A.M. shift. The company prospered under Fay Watson's careful watch, but after his death in 1958 no one knew much about Watson Bros. operations. In 1959 the two remaining brothers decided to sell out, and in February, 1960, Walnut Grove Products, Inc., the old-line Atlantic, Iowa, feedmaker purchased 64.5 per cent of the shares. The company stock was soon dispersed publicly, with 4,022 shareholders owning the 2,082,624 shares outstanding. The president of Walnut Grove Products, Everett A. Kelloway, foresaw great possibilities for the trucking business, and, in 1960, Walnut Grove purchased three forwarding companies. Imperial Casualty and Indemnity Company; Globe Freight Service; Trans-Reality, Inc.; Hawaiian Freight Forwarders, Ltd.; Merchants Carloading Co., Inc.; Flynn Forwarding Company; Globeco, Inc.; Globe Car Leasing Corporation; and Nebraska-Iowa Sales and Service Company were all affiliated with Watson Bros. at the end of 1960. Operating revenues totaled $38.0 million for the ten companies in 1960, and the net loss was $177,357. In 1961 still another forwarding company was acquired and combined with the three already owned to form Star Forwarders, Inc. Next trucking authority was sought.

Through an exchange of stock, the Wilson Truck Company, Inc. was acquired on January 20, 1962. Wilson Truck Company had been incorporated in Tennessee on Nov. 21, 1933 by H. C. and Jesse Wilson. By 1940 operating revenues were $491,437, and net income was $7,653. The two Wilsons were the only shareholders of record. Their authority covered 1,479 miles in Georgia, Tennessee, Kentucky, Illinois, and Missouri. Ten years later H. C. Wilson was sole owner; revenues had grown to $3,413,977; and net income had reached $302,177. During the 1950's the routes were extended to Charleston, S.C., and control was purchased by Bransford, Sharp & Co. of Nashville. Wilson Truck Company was a well-managed and successful line in 1962 when it was acquired by Watson Bros. Soon the firm's name was changed to Watson-Wilson Transportation System, Inc. The addition of the

Wilson authority to Watson Bros. produced one of the first transcontinental routes—from Charleston, S. C., to San Francisco, Calif.

In late 1962 Walnut Grove Products brought in an experienced transportation man as president of Watson-Wilson, but his efforts only partially succeeded. W. R. Grace & Company purchased Walnut Grove Products in 1964. It was stipulated that Watson-Wilson was to be sold immediately. The deal had to be quick which necessitated that a nontruck purchaser be involved in order to avoid Interstate Commerce Commission jurisdiction. Kelloway persuaded Gilbert Swanson of the Swanson Foods family to buy control of Watson-Wilson. The sale went through during August, 1964.

Soon after the takeover, Swanson realized that the problems at Watson-Wilson were deeper than he had thought, and he began a systematic search for a merger partner. Swanson, unlike his predecessors, looked for a trucking company partner. A New York bank brought Swanson and Yellow Freight System together, and in January, 1965, the details were worked out. On Mar. 2, 1965, the ICC granted temporary authority to Yellow Freight System for the management and operation of Watson-Wilson, and on Mar. 9 actual management by Yellow Freight System commenced.

Streamlining the Watson-Wilson operation became the immediate goal of Yellow Freight System. The two major divisions, the former Watson Bros. and Wilson Truck Co., had never really been integrated and great differences in approach existed. By Yellow Freight System standards, far too many solicitors were in the field looking for business. Cutbacks were instituted when and where possible. Watson-Wilson's on-time performance was low, about 25 per cent. Under Yellow Freight System guidance, the operation soon had surpassed the 75 per cent on-time mark. Improvements were apparent after only a few changes. During the first quarter of 1965, Watson-Wilson lost $593,000. During the second quarter, the first under Yellow Freight System's care, the loss was reduced to $269,000. This figure was still a long way from the record earnings made by Yellow Freight System itself, but the trend was definitely in the right direction. During the third quarter, a profit of $128,000 was earned. For the year, Watson-Wilson had a net loss of $563,266. The first six months of 1966 presented a reversed earnings picture: Watson-Wilson cleared $876,953 after taxes.

Permanent authority from the ICC for control of Watson-Wilson by the Yellow Freight System was required before Yellow could integrate

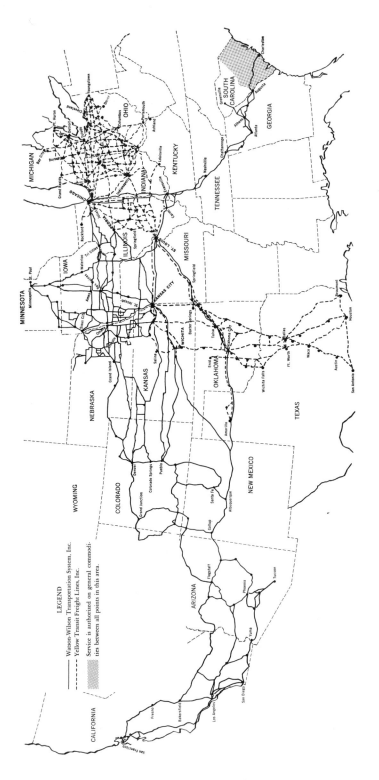

FIGURE 3

Principal Routes of Yellow Transit Freight Lines, Inc. and Watson-Wilson
Transportation System, Inc., 1966

the systems physically. Watson-Wilson appealed to Yellow primarily for its long West Coast hauls; duplication was at a minimum. Chicago, St. Louis, and Kansas City were the only major cities where both companies had terminals. Operating authorities overlapped into a small section—Evansville, Ind., to Wichita. The combined systems fitted together beautifully. The Yellow Freight System points east of St. Louis could feed the long routes west with the varied and heavy flow of manufactured products from Ohio, Michigan, Indiana, and Illinois. Extensive coverage of Iowa, Nebraska, Colorado, and southern Minnesota would be added to the Yellow Freight System, and finally the leg into the South and to the ocean at Charleston would make trucking operations coast to coast. (The principal routes of Yellow Freight System and Watson-Wilson are shown in Figure 3 as they were in 1966.)

The merger of Watson-Wilson Transportation Company and Yellow was expected to increase efficiency in combined operations through improved routing and scheduling. Also, management anticipated more efficient use of equipment and smoother office operations. In addition, personnel could be used more effectively in supervisory and sales work. Better service to the shipping public was also expected to result from the consolidation of the terminal facilities at Chicago, St. Louis, and Kansas City. Prompt consummation of the merger was planned after ICC approval was granted.

Included in the merger plan was a provision to change the name of the surviving corporation to Yellow Freight System, Inc.; Yellow Transit Freight Lines, Inc. simply did not describe the widened scope of transportation activity carried on by the company. Just as Yellow Cab Transit Company and Yellow Transit Company had outgrown their corporate titles, so did Yellow Transit Freight Lines. Because of the much wider scope of company activities, the name, Yellow Freight System, was adopted after the merger.

Yellow's initial concern in January, 1965, was to acquire sufficient Watson-Wilson stock ownership to constitute favorable control. Its first ICC application, therefore, asked authority to own stock but to delay merger. It was hoped that Watson-Wilson, as a separate corporation controlled by Yellow, could realize federal tax benefits by carrying forward losses. Also, in order to gain experience with a larger endeavor, Yellow management desired actual control of Watson-Wilson operations for a period of time before merging equipment, facilities, employees (including union seniority lists), and operating authorities. The ICC authorized Yellow Freight System to assume

temporary control of Watson-Wilson on Mar. 9, 1965, and this order
was to be in effect until June 24, 1966. When this proposed delay in
merger was included in the public announcements in March, 1965, a
group of investors, mostly in the Dallas, Texas, area, purchased
Watson-Wilson shares on the market, refraining, however, from joining in the agreement to sell to Yellow. In the aggregate, the group
acquired over 100,000 Watson-Wilson shares. Yellow's management
made improvements in the controlled Watson-Wilson operations. The
minority shareholders later protested the formal merger on the grounds
of alleged inadequacy of the proposed exchange basis. As a result of
this protest and the subsequent lawsuit, a compromise settlement with
the minority shareholders was reached. Decision in the control proceedings was delayed by the filing of various legal protests by other
motor carriers. After Yellow and the protestants reached a compromise agreement over operating rights, the protests were withdrawn,
and control conditions were established. On May 5, 1966, the ICC
granted authority for permanent control to become effective on June
24. By Sept. 12, 1966, Yellow Freight System owned all of the
1,342,848 Class B Watson-Wilson common shares and 1,070,720 of the
1,201,076 issued and outstanding Class A common shares (exclusive
of the 16,200 treasury shares).

Watson-Wilson operations and profits had been greatly improved
during the period of Yellow Freight System's temporary control. The
management personnel of Watson-Wilson had become almost exclusively Yellow Freight System people. The general offices of Watson-
Wilson at Omaha had been closed; the administrative and accounting
functions had been moved to Yellow Freight Systems offices in Kansas
City, Mo. Under the permanent control arrangement, Watson-Wilson
terminals in such widespread locations as Atlanta, Albuquerque, and
Los Angeles were soon staffed with Yellow Freight System managers.
In addition to supplying capable employees, Yellow Freight System
provided Watson-Wilson with working capital. By June 30, 1966,
$2,474,604 had been advanced on a noninterest bearing, open account.
Revenue equipment costing $800,000 was purchased by Yellow Freight
System's equipment and terminal subsidiary for lease to Watson-
Wilson, and terminals costing over $2,000,000 were constructed for
Watson-Wilson's use.

Yellow Freight System managers at Watson-Wilson instituted operating policies similar to Yellow's. For example, Watson-Wilson had
worked on a sleeper system, but, with the cooperation of the local
teamsters union organizations, the entire Watson-Wilson system was

converted to a slip-seat arrangement. Many union people were moved as a result of this change, but the union confidence that Yellow Freight System had gained over the years helped make the relocations and changeovers occur smoothly. Yellow and the entire motor carrier industry, were affected by the nationwide lockout and wildcat strikes involved in negotiations with the Teamsters' Union in 1967.

In anticipation of the eventual merger, which did not occur until December, 1968, Yellow management combined the functions of Yellow Transit Freight Lines, Watson-Wilson Transportation System, Yellow Forwarding, Star Forwarders, and their subsidiaries into several divisions. Separate corporate identity was maintained, but day-to-day operations were integrated by division as much as possible. Five divisions existed at the end of 1967.

General Commodities Division produced the major portion of total revenues. It consisted of the domestic freight business of Yellow Transit, Watson-Wilson, Yellow Forwarding, and Star Forwarding.

Steel Transport Division operated in Michigan, Ohio, Illinois, and Indiana from headquarters at Indianapolis. Steel, the primary commodity hauled, was transported in sheets, rolls, and bars from the mills to fabricating plants in the region. Automotive firms and suppliers were the chief customers for this division. Heavy-duty tractors and flat-bed trailers, often owned by the drivers, constituted the equipment used. These operators had been part of the Yellow service since the merger with Michigan Motor Freight Lines in 1957.

Defense Transport Division moved defense materials in volume or truckload quantities. Operating in the western half of the United States, this division, a former Watson-Wilson service, had its headquarters in Denver. Leased operators provided most of the linehaul transportation in this division.

Thermo Transport Division engaged in the moving of special products that required temperature control protection. Refrigerated and insulated trailers were used primarily to haul perishable food producers from the West Coast to the Midwest. The division was another former Watson-Wilson service, and Denver was the administrative headquarters.

Star International Division consisted of export-import operations of the Star Forwarders subsidiary of Watson-Wilson. The business of this division was the consolidation and movement of international traffic.

By the end of 1967 a subsidiary of Star Forwarders, Inc., Global Air Cargo, had offices in New York, Chicago, Kansas City, Houston, Los Angeles, and Honolulu. The Civil Aeronautics Board had granted Global Air Cargo air freight forwarder domestic and international authority.

The complicated corporate structure, which recalled the troubled period of 1952, was the result of the still-pending merger of Watson-

Wilson into Yellow. Three former Watson-Wilson subsidiaries, Globe Car Leasing Corporation; Trans-Reality, Inc.; and Globeco, Inc., had been dissolved on Sept. 28, 1966. Merger proceedings were grinding slowly. A group of shareholders, that held 5.76 per cent of the Watson-Wilson stock in late 1966, opposed the merger. The essential disagreement centered on the terms of exchange. The protesting group, almost all of whom acquired their Watson-Wilson shares subsequent to the original control agreement in 1965, sought substantially more favorable terms based on the improved condition of Watson-Wilson and the relative decline of Yellow caused by its takeover of Watson-Wilson. In other words, the substantial injection of capital and management by Yellow to rejuvenate Watson-Wilson led to a short-run period during which Yellow advanced less rapidly than Watson-Wilson and declined only in a relative sense. The ICC hearing examiner in his report and order filed Nov. 29, 1967, recommended that at the time of the merger the protesting Watson-Wilson shareholders receive for their shares the same consideration provided in the plan for nonprotestants.

Nevertheless, on Mar. 4, 1968, a minority stockholder representative civil action was filed in the U.S. District Court at Kansas City, Mo., against Yellow, Watson-Wilson, and three directors. The complaint alleged improper accounting between Watson-Wilson and Yellow and improper use and division of revenue, income, and assets of Watson-Wilson after Yellow had acquired temporary control. The complaint asked that $3,250,000 be paid to Watson-Wilson. The position of Yellow management was succinctly stated: the action was without merit.

Meanwhile, Yellow management continued to develop the system. During 1967 enlarged terminal facilities were completed in Los Angeles, Oakland, Nashville, and Atlanta on the Watson-Wilson routes, and at the joint terminals in Kansas City and St. Louis. On Sept. 21, 1967, the Board of Directors approved a plan for the purchase of operating authority for hauling explosives in California from Pacific Express Transportation and added the rights to the Watson-Wilson authorities. Revenue equipment expenditures for the Yellow Freight System totaled $14,342,000 in 1968 alone. The results were conspicuous. Revenues were $132,658,000 in 1968; 27 per cent higher than 1967. The 1968 net income of $7,031,000 was a 56 per cent jump over 1967.

Throughout 1968 all parties involved anxiously awaited the ICC resolution of the merger application, which hinged on the commission's decision on exceptions to an examiner's report. The ICC weighed the points of disagreement between the protestants and Yellow. The protestants charged Yellow's management with improper financial procedures between Watson-Wilson and Yellow. They sought a complete exchange of shares without a partial cash payment. Management maintained that the protestants were speculators and should be compensated in the same manner as nonprotestants. Management wished to settle in cash with the group. On this issue the commission noted:

> Speculation in stock may involve greater risks than ordinary investment, but it is lawful. Conversely, when Yellow acquired control of Watson, it properly instituted procedural and policy changes for the good of the system. Short of any attempt to defraud minority stockholders by "taking the gold out" of Watson, its efforts to make adjustments in intercorporate financial and operating arrangements are not evidence of questionable practices.[1]

On the question of exchange payment, the commission found a combination of 0.15 shares of Yellow for each share of Watson-Wilson plus a cash amount desirable. Experts on stock valuation testified, and not surprisingly the results were far apart. The expert of the protestants argued for a high Watson-Wilson value. The experts for Yellow Freight System found a low worth for Watson-Wilson.

The ICC combed the records and examined each of the intercorporate financial procedures. A write-down of Watson-Wilson operating equipment had occurred to bring the value in line with the then current market price. This was deemed improper by ICC accounting practices. Joint terminal and office expenses had been questioned by the protestants. On this issue the commission found no reason to change Yellow's partitions of the joint expenses. A change in the proration of interline revenues of 10 per cent in favor of Yellow on traffic moving between the two truck lines was reversed for valuation purposes. The commission noted the benefits that came to Watson-Wilson from Yellow's management talent. At the conclusion, the ICC engaged in the inexact art of establishing a per share cash value for a stock, more than 90 per cent of which is owned by another company. Commenting that they could appease either side only by setting stock values at the highest or lowest level, the commission chose a middle position. The

[1]Interstate Commerce Commission, "Yellow Transit Freight Lines, Inc.—Merger —Watson-Wilson Transportation System, Inc.," *Reports, Motor Carrier Cases*, CIV (Washington: U.S. Gov't Printing Office), p. 752.

0.15 shares of Yellow for 1.00 shares of Watson-Wilson was retained, but for their speculative activities the protestant group was given an additional $1.94 per Watson-Wilson share.

The entire exchange question became involved in the overlapping of jurisdiction in the regulation of the securities of motor common carriers. Nebraska, where Watson-Wilson was incorporated, had laws that were different from Indiana, where Yellow was incorporated. Cases were cited in which state laws were governing and in which ICC jurisdiction was final. The situation was an example of the several layers of governmental involvement in security regulation.[2] In this case the ICC claimed complete jurisdiction, however, and determined the final outcome.

The dissident Watson-Wilson shareholders were one of two groups protesting the merger. The second group involved employees at St. Louis. On Jan. 1, 1967, the Yellow and Watson-Wilson terminals were combined, with employees placed on a dovetailed seniority list. Twenty-two dock workers were laid off, but they all were rehired within three weeks. Some of the workers were lower on the list than formerly (when counted from the top), but by the time of the merger application hearing, more employees were below the protestants than before the dovetailing. The city drivers at St. Louis faced the same situation. The examiner in the merger application declined to consider this aspect because it fell within the previously settled control transaction of Watson-Wilson by Yellow. A solution was reached by reserving the jurisdiction for two years to protesting employees only. In that time period, the employees could be granted appropriate relief if they were affected adversely.[3] Disagreements of this sort grew out of the acquisition of the entire corporate entity of Watson-Wilson Transportation System and all of its property.

The ICC report emerged on Oct. 10, 1968. In early December, 1968, the ICC granted final approval on all conditions of the merger, and on Dec. 9 merger was formally accomplished. The Watson-Wilson Transportation System, which at one time had been the larger concern in terms of revenues, was included in the then officially named Yellow Freight System, Inc.

[2]Leslie W. Jacobs, "Second Thoughts: Regulation of Securities of Inter-city Motor Common Carriers of Property," *Ohio State Law Journal* (Winter, 1969), pp. 84-130.
[3]Interstate Commerce Commission, "Yellow Transit Freight Lines, Inc.—Merger —Watson-Wilson Transportation System, Inc.," pp. 743-44.

Simplification of the corporate structure occurred promptly. The eight subsidiaries existing at the end of 1967 were reduced to six by the end of 1968. The several divisions existing at the end of 1967 had been consolidated into two divisions, General Freight Division and the Special Hauling Division, by late 1968. The Special Hauling Division carried truckload traffic requiring special services and hauling with most of the linehaul transportation provided by leased operators.

The merger had taken almost four years from contract signing in February, 1965, to the consumation in December, 1968. Unpleasant legal entanglements had marred and slowed the proceedings. The long period, however, provided ample time for the removal of assimilation problems that often occur after a merger. By December, 1968, Yellow Freight System, Inc. was set for a new challenge.

12 / Toward Nationwide Coverage

With the completion of the merger with Watson-Wilson Transportation System and with the constant improvement of the combined operations, Yellow's management began to contemplate additional route authorities to round out the system. Due to its success, Yellow Freight System was beginning to attract other companies that were having difficulties. Yellow found itself sought as a takeover partner. This chapter traces the acquisitions and growth that has occurred since 1968.

DEFENSE MATERIALS

During the Korean War, the old Yellow Transit Freight Lines had engaged in hauling defense materials, primary explosives. As long as the volume was high, the extra attention necessary to attract and then to truck such materials proved profitable. Yet, as the volume tendered for shipment dropped after the conflict, Yellow Transit found the burden of special handling excessive, and the service was phased out. From time to time in the past other special haul experiments were undertaken, such as a bulk flour scheme, but only the steel hauling portion of the Yellow Transit operation lasted as a special hauling division.

Watson-Wilson, on the other hand, possessed extensive explosives authority in the Midwest and West. As a result, at the time of the control of Watson-Wilson, Yellow Freight System once again became an explosives hauler. For about three years following the takeover the defense transport division continued to prosper. In 1967 negotiations with Pacific Express Transportation were opened for the purchase of explosive rights in the San Francisco Bay and Los Angeles areas. Approval became final in 1969. Also in 1969 explosive rights in Indiana and Illinois, essentially from Crane, Ind., to Joliet, Ill., were acquired from Transport Motor Express, Inc. of Fort Wayne, Ind. By the time these transfers were final, their worth was small.

American Farm Lines and similar exempt cooperatives had diverted the explosives traffic from regulated carriers. Until about 1966, the clash between agricultural cooperatives and the carriers regulated by the ICC had been minimal. Motor vehicles controlled and operated by cooperative associations as defined in the Agricultural Marketing Act or those controlled and operated by a federation of cooperatives were specifically excluded from regulation. The commonly held view had been that the exemption did not permit the cartage of nonmember freight. A 1965 court decision, *Northwest Agricultural Cooperatives Ass'n. v. Interstate Commerce Commission*, radically altered that interpretation of the limitations, and freight that was incidental to the cooperatives service began to be transported for nonmembers. Basically, the problem arose from the desire of the cooperatives to fill their back-haul moves. This activity was the crux of the court decision.

Soon the U.S. Department of Defense began using exempt cooperatives to haul explosives. The nonregulated status of the cooperatives provided them with freedom to charge any rate and to travel over irregular routes. American Farm Lines, one of these cooperative marketing organizations, jumped into the munitions trade and grew rapidly, at the expense of the regulated carriers. The growth of the transportation of nonmember traffic by the cooperatives led to a change in 1968 in the exemption provision of the federal law. The nonmember, nonfarm related transportation was limited to 15 per cent of the total tonnage of the cooperatives. American Farm Lines filed for temporary and permanent authority to continue its explosives hauling. Despite evidence suggesting the harm done to common carriage by such operations, Division 1 of the ICC granted temporary authority; its decision was eventually upheld in the courts. Permanent authority had not been settled by 1970.

For Yellow Freight System the result of the American Farm Lines controversy was the loss of the explosives traffic. This loss meant that the newly purchased and previously owned operating authorities were no longer very useful for the company. Once again explosives ceased to contribute to the traffic on the Yellow Freight System.

LOCAL AREA ACQUISITIONS

In October, 1968, Race Motor Service, Inc. and its subsidiary, Fleet Services, Inc., both Illinois corporations, were purchased for $254,000. Approval from the ICC was immediately requested. Temporary authority was soon granted, and in April, 1970, the two companies with headquarters at Blue Island, Ill., became part of the Yellow Freight System, Inc. An attractive blanket authority to all points within a 50 mile radius of Chicago was acquired through the purchase. All assets and land of the firms were also acquired. Yellow recognized the growing importance of outlying manufacturing centers in the Chicago area when it made the Race purchase.

In December, 1968, two months after the announcement of Race negotiations, Yellow Freight System, Inc. concluded an agreement to acquire the Red Arrow Transportation Company, Inc. Temporary operating authority was approved in January, 1969, with permanent acquisition in 1970. Red Arrow originally had been founded as Missouri-Arkansas Transportation Co. and had long faced financial difficulties. It had operated since 1937 but went bankrupt in July, 1968. The company served the territory in southwest Missouri, northwest Arkansas, northeast Oklahoma, and southeast Kansas. Fort Smith and Springdale, Ark., became terminal points on the system, and such Kansas communities as Columbus were added as service points.

The next addition to the system occurred in March, 1969, with the purchase of the outstanding shares of stock in the Lang Transit Company of Lubbock, Tex. The Lang authority had been pieced together during the 1950's and 1960's and covered the area from Amarillo and Lubbock, Tex., to Hobbs and Clovis, N. M. Lubbock became a terminal location after the acquisition. The intrastate rights of Lang were sold by Yellow, but fortunately for those interested in colorful names, Muleshoe, Tex., remained a service point on the system.

Traffic from the southeastern area of the United States that was hauled by Yellow Freight System to the Southwest and West moved through the St. Louis gateway under Yellow's operating authority. In late 1969 closed-door authority across Arkansas on Interstate 40 was requested under the Superhighway and Deviation Rules. These rules contain three restrictions: (1) the requested authority cannot be less than 85 per cent of authorized mileage; or (2) the requested authority must be within 25 airline miles of the current authorization; or (3) no protest can be registered within 30 days after notice of intention. No protest was filed, and Yellow's drivers began to move from Nashville through Memphis and Little Rock to Fort Smith where a second driver took the load through Oklahoma City to Amarillo where the freight moved into the system for ultimate delivery. Although the Yellow Freight System trucks were thus on the highways around Memphis and Little Rock, the two cities were not service points under the closed-door rights.

In 1970 service in the Fresno, Calif., area was increased by the addition of the American Cartage Co. authority in Tulare, Madera, Kings, and Fresno counties. The company had been started in 1961 as H. McBride Delivery Service and was sold to American Cartage on the death of the founder, Harold H. McBride. Extensive coverage of the central San Joaquin Valley was added by this purchase, which was approved by the ICC in 1970. Yellow agreed to purchase all of the outstanding capital stock of the Scott Transportation Co., which was situated farther south in the Los Angeles basin area. The offer was extended in February, 1970, and ICC approval was granted in May, 1971. The exchange was made for $186,000 cash. Scott operating rights added such cities as Barstow, Redlands, Riverside, and San Bernardino to the Yellow Freight System.

Some acquisition possibilities were rejected by the board of directors. The company had decided in April, 1968, that a systematic approach to mergers was necessary for careful and proper growth. One type of addition was the sort the Race, Red Arrow, Lang, American Cartage, and Scott authorities provided. These lines were small, and their purchase tended to round out the Yellow Freight System in particular areas. The magnitude of the potential revenue and income additions were such that acquisition with cash on hand was approved by the board. Some of the lessons of the large-scale Watson-Wilson merger added an element of caution to other large merger ventures, and no mergers were approved during 1968. In May, 1969, the board of directors was presented a plan to purchase a portion of the operating authority of a large Eastern carrier. This was a different ball game.

THE NORWALK PURCHASE

The operating authorities offered to Yellow Freight System included some of the rights of the Norwalk subsidiaries of United-Buckingham Freight Lines, Inc. The Norwalk properties were part of what had been an old and proud motor carrier, The Norwalk Truck Line Company, at one time one of the nation's largest. The firm had been incorporated in Ohio on Jan. 15, 1923, by John Ernsthausen, who had been in the produce business. Ernsthausen found the service on the Lake Shore Electric Railway inadequate, and in 1921 a group of associates proposed to truck the Norwalk Produce Co. products to Cleveland. By 1924 the results were so satisfying that the company was founded and incorporated early the next year. Through the 1920's and 1930's route authorities were added until in 1940, 2,663 miles were covered. By 1955 the mileage had increased to 4,264, and the geographic coverage extended from Pittsburgh to Chicago with intensive coverage of northern Ohio, northern Indiana, and southern Michigan.

The Norwalk Truck Line Co. had grown and prospered as a short haul carrier featuring excellent service. John Ernsthausen's life had been his truckline, and he had managed it well. About the time of his sixty-fifth birthday, in 1953, he devised a plan whereby the employees of the firm became the owners at his death. His idea was to perpetuate ownership and control within the administrative personnel of Norwalk. That part of his plan succeeded, but soon after Ernsthausen's death the employee group started expansion plans.

In 1957 Norwalk Truck Line Co., the Ohio concern, acquired control of Shirks Motor Express Corporation. Shirks had been incorporated in Delaware in 1935 to serve the area from Baltimore to Rochester and Lancaster to Cleveland. By 1950 the system had been extended to Philadelphia, New York, Buffalo, and Alexandria. At the time of the Norwalk take-over, revenues had reached $11 million a year. Norwalk changed the Shirks name to Norwalk Truck Lines, Inc. of Delaware and operated the two companies as a single system. For a few years the Norwalk companies prospered, and additional Illinois and Wisconsin points were added to the system. Operations failed to achieve expectations, however, and by 1965 trouble was evident. In that year a holding company, Nortruk, Inc., was incorporated in Delaware to acquire the capital stock of the operating companies. Operating revenues of Nortruk and its subsidiaries totaled some $52 million in 1966, but the performance of the operating companies varied from loss to profit. The system was not running smoothly. In 1967 control of Nortruk, and through it the operating subsidiaries, was acquired by United-Buckingham Freight Lines, Inc. Although United-Buckingham had hoped to realize economies and improvements in the Norwalk operations through both operational changes and replacement of equipment, the efforts proved ineffective. After almost two years of United-Buckingham control, the Norwalk companies had lost in excess of $3 million. The entire United-Buckingham system was shaken.

In early May, 1969, officials of Ringsby Truck Lines, Inc. contacted Yellow Freight System officials to report that Ringsby had made an agreement to purchase control of United-Buckingham Freight Lines, Inc. The Ringsby interest did not include the eastern authorities and operations of the Norwalk companies that were under United-Buckingham control. These rights, which covered the area encompassed by Cleveland and Youngstown, Ohio; Springfield, Mass.; New York City; Philadelphia; Baltimore; and Washington, D.C., were offered to Yellow Freight System, Inc. for cash. United-Buckingham had drained its resources in operating the eastern properties of the Norwalk system, and Ringsby, in the agreement to buy control, declined purchase of these properties. Yellow expressed interest, and a meeting was held in Kansas City on May 15, 1969. On May 29, 1969, a written contract between Yellow and the Norwalk companies was executed. This contract was entirely independent of arrangements or agreements with other motor carriers. The contract Yellow signed with the Norwalk companies, to be approved by all interested parties such as Ringsby and United-Buckingham, was designed so that the purchase could be carried out regardless of the results of efforts by others to acquire control of parent corporations of the Norwalk companies or to dispose of other Norwalk rights and properties. In other words, the entanglements were typical of faltering motor carrier systems and Yellow management wanted to avoid a recurrence of some of their previous experiences with companies in trouble.

Yellow Freight System agreed in the May 29 contract to pay $187,500 for the operating rights—extending from Cleveland to the Ohio-Pennsylvania state line—of Norwalk Truck Lines, Inc., the Ohio Company. Common points with Yellow were Cleveland, Warren, Niles, and Salem, Ohio. These operating rights connected with the authority of the Norwalk Truck Lines, Inc. of Delaware at six points on the state boundary between East Liverpool, Ohio, and Lake Erie. All of the Norwalk of Delaware authority was included in the transaction except for an irregular route between Cleveland and points in Ohio within 130 miles south and east of Cleveland. The price of these rights was fixed at $1,812,500. The Norwalk of Delaware rights provided extensive coverage of New York, Pennsylvania, and New Jersey, and lesser coverage of Massachusetts, Connecticut, Delaware,

Maryland, Virginia, and the District of Columbia. Terminal points added to the motor carrier operation of the Yellow Freight System were the following:

Albany, N. Y.	New York, N. Y.
Allentown, Pa.	North Bergen, N. J.
Baltimore, Md.	Philadelphia. Pa.
Bloomsburg, Pa.	Pittsburgh, Pa.
Buffalo, N. Y.	Rochester, N. Y.
Edison, N. J.	Scranton, Pa.
Elmira, N. Y.	Springfield, Mass.
Erie, Pa.	Syracuse, N. Y.
Lancaster, Pa.	Wilmington, Del.

The terminals included in the purchase contract were all located in Pennsylvania: Greenville, Butler, Lancaster, and Philadelphia. The Lancaster terminal still retained the former Shirks name. Upon investigation it was discovered that the Norwalk companies did not possess a legal title to the Philadelphia terminal, and it could not be acquired. Other operating property and leases and certain terminal leases were assumed by the Yellow Freight System at an additional expense to the price for the operating authority. The total transaction involved about $8.0 million, but no stock exchange or issuance was included. Application for temporary operating authority was approved by the ICC, and actual operation began July 14, 1969.

On July 14, 1969, all Norwalk employees except at Cleveland and Warren, Ohio, were placed on the Yellow payroll. At Cleveland and Warren a number of Norwalk employees transferred to the Yellow facility at West Richfield, Ohio. These changes occurred after consultation with, and approval of, the local unions involved. The West Richfield terminal was added to the Yellow Freight System at that time. The new location provided a new local pickup and delivery point for Cleveland, a break-bulk terminal for the Norwalk operation, and a relay point for Norwalk.

The region in which the Norwalk properties were located had been known among truckers as a high-cost territory. Some questioned the desirability of Yellow's moving into the area. Yellow Freight System had been familiar with many of the Eastern markets since 1960 when the company that became Yellow Forwarding Co. was acquired. The Norwalk purchase was, then, the addition of highway authority to serve the same markets. Yellow was able to introduce the flexibility of its own motor carrier operation into its forwarder territory and at the same time control the line-haul costs. An attractive element in the takeover was the opportunity to expand and to improve service to existing customers of the Yellow Freight System. In addition, since Yellow had been participating in east coast traffic on an interline basis, the acquisition offered an opportunity for single-line service. The severe operational problems of the Norwalk companies would have to be solved, but Yellow had turned profits from other troubled carriers. If Yellow could meet the challenge, the market offered phenomenal growth potential.

During the remainder of 1969 the Norwalk operation was converted to the Yellow Freight System program of operation. In the Oct. 14, 1969, third quarter report to shareholders, Yellow management indicated about a $0.12 per share adverse effect on earnings as the result of Norwalk operations, a total of approximately $420,000. At the end of the year the loss figures were $700,000, or $0.20 per share. By the time of the third quarter report on Oct. 12, 1970, the trend had begun to be favorable, and the Norwalk operation had made a satisfactory profit contribution.

In addition to the West Richfield terminal, which had been extensively rehabilitated, the Norwalk purchase led to construction projects at several other locations. At the end of 1970 new facilities had been completed at Baltimore, Philadelphia, and Springfield, Mass. The Special Hauling Division was enlarged by expansion into the Norwalk regions of Pennsylvania and New York. The Yellow operation of Norwalk companies had strengthened, expanded, and improved service to customers not only in the Norwalk area but also in the entire Yellow Freight System area. By December, 1970, the ICC had approved the acquisition except for the route segment into Massachusetts, which was held for further consideration. In 1971 that addition was approved also.

ADDITIONAL GROWTH

The one area of the eastern seaboard served by Yellow Forwarding Co. but not included in the Norwalk motor carrier surface rights was the area from Boston to New York City. Several significant manufacturing centers are located here, and Yellow Freight System management was anxious to connect such cities as Bridgeport, New Haven, Worcester, and Boston with the transcontinental routes of Yellow. New York and Worcester Express Co. possessed authority in the area, and in 1970 an offer of $200,000 was extended. In May, 1971, ICC approval was granted; thus, New York and Worcester became part of Yellow Freight System.

The remaining largest city and manufacturing area in the United States not served by Yellow Freight System was Milwaukee. Curiously, Milwaukee was a service point of a truckline purchased by the Yellow Transit Company. In 1941 the Ethington Freight Lines of Mattoon, Ill., had been acquired by A. J. Harrell, but he persuaded Ernest Ethington to retain certain limited rights including those to Milwaukee. Since Milwaukee was located less than 100 miles from Chicago, Yellow's expansion to it was quite natural. In early 1971 an agreement was signed with Yule Truck Lines, Inc. for purchase of its interstate rights and those of its subsidiary, Hill Freight Lines, Inc. The price was $300,000 cash. The Wisconsin cities of Milwaukee, Racine, and Kenosha plus a terminal at LaSalle, Ill., were added to the Yellow Freight System under temporary authority granted by the ICC in May, 1971.

Terminal facilities required constant improvement and expansion with the growing system. In addition to those added and enlarged in former Norwalk territory, during fiscal year 1969-70 new buildings and additions were completed at Amarillo and Austin, Tex.; Rockford, Ill.; Muncie, Ind.; Port Huron, Grand Rapids, and Marshall, Mich.; Augusta, Ga.; Greenville and Sumpter, S. C.; and Minneapolis, St. Paul, Minn. At the end of 1970 Yellow Freight System terminals and offices were located in 115 cities in 31 states and Canada. Figure 4 shows the complete Yellow Freight System as it appeared in early 1971.

Not all of the geographic expansion has occurred in the motor carrier operation. In August, 1970, a Yellow Forwarding Co. terminal was opened in El Paso, Tex., for inbound forwarder traffic. For overseas traffic, the Star International segment of the Yellow Freight System handled import-export and Hawaiian traffic in containers moving via rail and water. The principal operation had occurred between Chicago and St. Louis, on the one hand, and Hawaii and Europe, on the other. The small Star operation enabled Yellow Freight System to participate in a freight transportation market with all appearances of growth potential. In early 1971 Star International established through container service from either Chicago or St. Louis—with single carrier responsibility and without transfer of lading—via the port of New York to Rotterdam. By participating in new shipping patterns, Star was in a position to grow as new traffic developed.

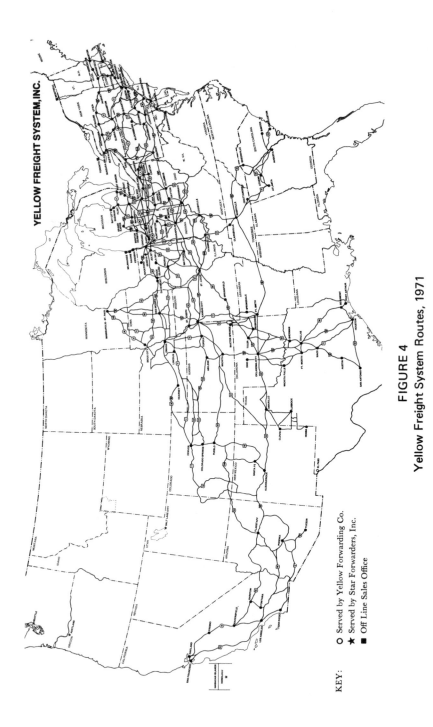

FIGURE 4

Yellow Freight System Routes, 1971

Chapter 12 has traced the acquisitions and concomitant added routes and physical facilities to the Yellow Freight System since the Watson-Wilson merger of 1968. This tremendous growth of the company resulted in more people who needed office space at headquarters. The executive office building of the company at 92nd Street and State Line Road in Kansas City, first occupied in 1960, was a large two-story building with three one-story wings. With future office space in mind, the designers had made provision for the addition of a third floor. Although completion of the addition was delayed until January, 1970, by one of the periodic Kansas City construction strikes, some personnel did move into the east end of the third floor almost ten years to the day after the building had been originally occupied. The west wing executive suite, the furnishings for which were selected by Mrs. George E. Powell, Jr., was done in a Spanish colonial motif that complemented the company and blended with the Spanish flavor in other areas of Kansas City.

13 | Solving the Problems of Size

Transportation companies, because their personnel are geographically dispersed, have long recognized the necessity of personnel policies that ensure equal treatment for and awareness of all their employees. Seniority systems were an approach to the problem. A straight time-in-service scheme seldom results in an effective management and work-force team, and shortly after acquiring control of the company in 1952, Yellow managers realized that other methods had to be tried also. By 1956 a full-time executive position had been created to deal with personnel matters. Once the procedures were instituted and all was running smoothly, and the personnel functions had become a part of the standard work of all supervisory people, managerial talent was freed for use in other areas. Since the company was small and had an exceptional esprit de corps, responsibility divided among many worked adequately. Then the Yellow Freight System began to mushroom. Revenues in 1956 had been $12.4 million; in 1966 the figure was $104.6 million. A full-time director of personnel was added in July, 1966.

The functions of the director of personnel were not established to remove responsibility from those in the field. Rather, the position was created to coordinate, formulate, and moderate those staff duties normally assigned to a personnel office. Development of a consistent policy on hiring was the first job undertaken. By 1970 about 8,000 persons were employed by Yellow Freight System, and qualifications for the many jobs they held were remarkably varied. Thus, guidelines for employment were essential, and specifications were set up for each slot. Uniformity of treatment for all employees was one important facet of these new policies. The hiring of general office personnel became a second immediate task of the director. Yellow had always attracted high quality employees with good working conditions and commensurate pay. A set of well-defined standards for employment and an effective applicant screening procedure helped to maintain and to raise that quality.

The minority employee program of the company was also assigned to the director of personnel. Since Yellow Freight System operated over an extensive geographic area, a significant number of minority groups were involved. The personnel staff drew up a coordinated plan for attracting minority group employees. A program whereby these employees could develop their individual talents was also organized. Reporting to governmental agencies on the status of the various minority group projects (often very arduous) was also the responsibility of the personnel staff.

The administration of company benefit plans was another major area in personnel. To encourage a closer working relationship among the employees, a profit-sharing trust was established as part of the package of employee benefits in 1962. The plan allowed certain employees to participate in the trust following one year of employment. The first actual investment occurred on Jan. 1 of the second year. Participation in the fund has tended to encourage greater involvement in the company and therefore greater concern for each task. Each year—believing that improved earnings should directly benefit employees—the company has allocated a percentage of earnings to the trust fund. To ensure that the incentive has been adequate, the company allocations have been as generous as 15 per cent in 1968 and 10 per cent in 1970. Other portions of the benefit plan included group life, accidental death, and dismemberment insurance, medical expense benefits, disability absence benefits, and retirement benefits. The company pension plan was paid for entirely by Yellow Freight System. As in other companies, the employee benefits were available to the monthly rated employees not receiving benefits through collective bargaining agreements.

Another program delegated to the personnel staff was the Yellow educational financial assistance plan for permanent full-time employees. One goal of the educational assistance plan was to help employees complete their college education. Another goal was to help employees take individual courses. An employee was allowed to take a college course if it met the following conditions: (1) direct relationship to job assignment, (2) direct relationship to the next highest job classification, (3) credit toward the educational requirements of the current position, or (4) credit toward a degree or certificate.

The continued growth of Yellow Freight System led to the creation of a second position closely related to director of personnel, that of director of management development. One of the major projects undertaken by the director was the supervisory training and educational program. This program was designed in 1969 after information was gathered through extensive field projects. Two surveys, one of general employee attitudes and the other of employee knowledge of fringe benefits, were made through questionnaires and visits in the field. As an unexpected benefit, the surveys even helped to inform employees about company policies. Termination questionnaires were given to departing employees and mailed to recently separated persons. Divisional and regional managers were solicited for ideas. Summer employees were questioned about their impressions of the company. A survey of the presently employed supervisory force was also conducted. An interesting conclusion drawn from the surveys made by the director of management development was the disturbing one that better supervisory selection techniques were needed at the first line level. Turnover from discharge was above the level desired, and it occurred in a short time span. The problem appeared to be polarized; that is, either excellent selections or poor ones were occurring. As a result supervisory selection training was instituted. A tightening-up of procedures, as well as instituting quality measures for new employees to be hired, helped solve the problem.

Another result of these surveys was the supervisory training and education program, which was designed to:

1. Provide managers additional skills for handling the complex problems of the present and future;

2. Congregate the supervisors of the company in a classroom atmosphere away from the terminals to learn, to know each other better, and to relax—in short, to create team spirit;

3. Establish in the supervisory personnel the significance of their performance on company success;

4. Provide top management an opportunity to assess the managerial talent of the supervisory group.

During the first two years a series of one-day meetings were held in 12 locations throughout the country. A total of 1,399 managers attended the meetings, which covered topics ranging from freight bill control procedures to leadership techniques. Each participant was presented a certificate of completion. After the meetings, programmed texts were sent to the managers; the texts more completely delved into the topics covered and related matters. A continuing series of meetings was planned for further development of managerial skills. Since the training and education programs were to be continuous, its evaluation had to be considered over time. The initial reports indicated a remarkable team spirit among the participating managers.

Several publications grew out of these personnel programs and served as an integral part of the personnel functions. The publication "STEP" emerged from the series of supervisory training and educational programs. The "STEP" newsletter featured items of interest to all employees and kept Yellow supervisory personnel informed of company developments and staff benefits—and for added interest a column on company "who's doing what" was included. A second bimonthly publication, "Yellow Freight System. Inc., NEWS," was started in May, 1971, for all regular employees. A quarterly magazine for company employees and share holders was first circulated in July, 1971. A periodical adjunct to this book, the magazine was entitled *Yellow in Motion.*

The programs of the personnel and management development staffs were beneficial for employees and supervisors at all levels within the organization. Newly hired persons adapted to the working environment quickly because issues, standards, and expectations were spelled out more clearly than they previously had been. At the middle management level, where an infusion of college-trained people was desired, some diffferent problems were evident. Transportation in general, and trucking in particular, has not been a field that has attracted college graduates in more than modest numbers. On the other hand, the corps of college students interested in transportation has been a dedicated lot. For some time Yellow Freight System had tried to recruit able college graduates. Yellow's newly implemented personnel policies in this area achieved the aims of the company by 1970. The program of individualized training periods established in the early 1960's to bring young people from within the company and from colleges and universities into middle management ranks was succeeding. The low turnover rate was evidence of the program's success, but perhaps more significant was the foundation for the future it built. Visiting colleges to discuss Yellow Freight with interested graduating seniors or master's candidates became part of the personnel function in the mid-1960's. At first the schools selected were those in the geographic area of Kansas City and those with whom the company had developed a working relationship. After the director of management development was appointed, a more ambitious college recruiting program was instituted, with recruiters visiting schools across the country. Since continuing relations with particular schools and the students attending them required a great deal of effort, Yellow attempted to select a few schools, become well-known at the institutions, and recruit high-quality people from them. In the long run this approach was thought to produce the best results.

EQUIPMENT, LABOR, DAMAGE, AND SAFETY

Equipment

The vast growth in Yellow Freight System in the 1965-71 period created a large capital need to purchase equipment, terminals, and other assets. From 1965 to 1970 new capital invested in equipment totaled $60 million. In some of the acquisitions rolling stock was included, as in the Watson-Wilson merger and Race purchase. In others, such as the Norwalk authority purchase, only selected property and equipment were acquired. Simply to meet the demands of the newly added business, substantial revenue producing equipment was needed. In addition, the traditional Yellow frequent replacement program was continued. The turnover of equipment on a systematic plan was, in effect, a substitution of capital for labor and had proven profitable. That is, rolling equipment was traded in before heavy maintenance and repair were necessary. The plan also allowed Yellow to profit from the latest models of equipment. This practice became particularly significant with the large-scale introduction of two shorter trailers in pairs, the so-called double-bottoms. By 1970 over half of the trailers owned by Yellow Freight System were the 27-foot lengths used in pairs. The added flexibility and reduced freight handling allowed by the double-bottoms resulted in improved efficiency.

All equipment was equally maintained and replaced, and innovations in all kinds of equipment were also given consideration. For instance, the operations manager at St. Louis devised a small, four-wheel mini-dolly used to move unattached converter dollies. With an investment of millions in tires alone, this aspect of rolling stock deserved special treatment. Thus, company meetings devoted to tire use and abuse were held in Kansas City. Department of Transportation tire regulations were explained, and other general topics concerning tires were discussed. Yellow's company experience still showed that recaps were not a good buy. Two disadvantages of using recapped tires were cited: frequent need to repair or replace recaps, with the attendant labor costs and down time involved, and the tendency of recaps to run somewhat hotter. Proper maintenance of tires was outlined to cope with Minnesota winters and Arizona summers. With a tire population of 43,000 tires, policies were critical. The system of tire banks maintained for several years had been improved so that no rig was ever more than 70 miles from a service point. The company was experimenting with improved methods of shipping tires throughout the system. For example, containerized racks were being considered because single tires have long been easy prey for pilferers.

Labor

The increasing size of Yellow also accentuated the trauma that occurred every three years during the contract negotiations with the Teamsters Union. At the expiration of the previous contract on March 31, 1970, a long period of work stoppage occurred, extending until July 3. The union president James R. Hoffa had succeeded by 1966 in achieving a national trucking agreement. But this agreement had one flaw: Chicago Truck Drivers, Helpers and Warehousemen's Union abstained from inclusion in the agreement. In 1967 and in 1970 the Chicago truckers won a higher raise than was negotiated nationally. A national agreement was tentatively reached on April 1, 1970, and the new contract called for a $1.10 per hour raise over a period of 39 months. The Chicago locals refused to ratify the contract, and eventually made their own settlement for $1.65 per hour over 36 months, about a 40 per cent increase. Since the national contract had specified a complete renegotiation if any company granted larger increases to a local union, the national contract was redone. The Chicago locals had succeeded in holding out for substantially higher increases. The labor costs for individual companies were only partially offset by rate increases, and many small truckers were reportedly closed out by the increases. Moreover, the costs of the disruption of service were substantial. The strikes closed several Yellow Freight System terminals for varying lengths of time. Most severe were the following: Oakland, 16 days; Akron, 27 days; Cleveland, 30 days;

St. Louis, 37 days; Los Angeles, 47 days; and the four Chicago area terminals, 87 days. The single bright spot in the contract settlement was the chance to look forward to three years of stable labor conditions.

A secondary labor problem that affected Yellow and other truckers in 1970 was a seven-week strike by steel haulers, ending the last of May. The strike was violent enough in some areas of Ohio and Pennsylvania, to warrant calling out the National Guard. In part, the pay increases that accrued to the steel haulers through increased steel freight rates were at stake. Typically, the steel haulers own their own rigs and split the revenues on a 75-25 basis with the companies for whom they haul. In addition, a $150 federal highway use tax was a point of contention. A concrete gain for the steel haulers was made when the companies assumed the tax payment. This action, of course, constituted an added cost for Yellow. A continuing problem for Yellow and other truckers was the dissatisfaction with Teamster representation, which was also another reason for the 1970 steel haulers' strike.

Damage

A steadily mounting problem in the motor carrier industry has been cargo losses through theft and pilferage. The 1970 strikes that idled loaded trailers encouraged this illegal activity. Estimates have indicated that loss from theft was 27 per cent higher in 1970 than in 1965. This problem has become more severe as Yellow has grown. From 1969 to 1970 the dollar value of claims from all causes jumped 66 per cent. Organized thievery plagued Yellow, as it did other companies. To combat this trend, Yellow was forced to increase internal security measures. A closely related problem, damage, also had to be given added attention. No major fires such as the devasting Dallas fire of Christmas, 1956, have marred the record, but serious fires have occurred. In February, 1971, fire hit at Indianapolis, destroying some freight there. Accidents have increased in number as the company has grown, resulting in added damage claims, but the frequency has not risen, which indicates an effective safety program.

Safety

To maintain this good safety record, the director of safety at Yellow Freight System administered a comprehensive program of accident prevention. Branch managers were responsible for the instruction, training, and supervision of all employees in the proper and safe use of equipment. The manager's job was also to see that the proper equipment was provided. Data processing equipment was used to devise complete records on each driver, freight handler, and shop employee, including his vehicle accident record, injury record, safety award record, physical examination record, and other pertinent information. Each terminal and division received a monthly report showing the number of accidents by road and by city drivers, as well as employee injuries. The frequency rate for the company was included for comparison. All traffic law infractions were investigated and corrective steps taken. The company also sponsored safety contests, with the terminals grouped by size. The branch manager had direct safety responsibility; the director of safety at the general office was charged with overall supervision and policy making. He frequently used "STEP" to distribute his messages and information. Yellow personnel were also active in the industry-wide trucking organizations, thereby benefiting from the exchange of information and helpful devices employed in other concerns.

THE SALES FUNCTIONS

The company's doubling in size during the 1965-70 period greatly affected the sales and marketing efforts of the company. As the number of terminals and sales offices increased, the sales force naturally expanded. Soon the vice-president of sales had a very large staff in the field. The central sales efforts at Yellow have traditionally been a staff function. The home office developed and established sales programs and goals, but the branch manager had direct responsibility for sales force employees. As the company grew, the need arose for carefully designed material that indicated Yellow services. For example, when Yellow served the area from Cleveland and Port Huron to Amarillo and San Antonio, the salesman in Grand Rapids had little difficulty in remembering precisely what services Yellow offered. The addition of points in Tennessee, Georgia, South Carolina, Colorado, New Mexico, Arizona, California, and Hawaii complicated this process. More significantly, shippers needed information on the services offered. To accommodate both the shippers and sales personnel a loose-leaf comprehensive guide to the services available was published by the company. The results of the carefully prepared and executed sales program could be seen in the former Norwalk territory. Soon after the purchase of the Norwalk companies the Yellow forwarding revenues from that area dropped, but, due to the efforts of the sales department, in a short time the total business generated in this same area substantially increased.

The sales function in transportation companies has often been relegated to second place, at least in the minds of operating personnel. This may be the result of the transportation product being a service. It may also be the result of a division of sales and operations in many transportation companies. The Yellow Freight System organizational structure, which has kept sales, operations, and all other responsibilities at the terminal level with staff support at the general office, has produced a unique strength in the sales area. The fact that a salesman in the field has been able to be the representative of the company to the shippers has resulted in efficiency seldom found in the industry. Equally important has been the support of the office of the vice-president of sales at the general office. The company structure, the efficient procedures, and the carefully planned goals were all necessary conditions for success.

CENTRAL DISPATCH

Through the years the additions to the Yellow Freight System were visible in the expansion of the Central Dispatch Office (CDO). By 1970 the CDO was housed in its own wing of the building. The CDO has been the nerve center of the company, and the imagination and skill of its staff were instrumental in designing the round-the-clock operations that directed the movement of vehicles over the entire system. Leased telephone lines and computer connections at each terminal were used to transmit the information exchange. When the general office building was occupied in 1960 the CDO personnel came up with the idea of a clear plastic board with holes in which small square plastic pieces representing trailers could be placed. The color of the squares and their location on the board provided quick information on the status of all trailers in the system. The range of knowledge required to work the CDO board probably qualified the CDO as the best on-the-spot training ground in Yellow Freight System.

INFORMATION SYSTEMS AND COMMUNICATIONS

The quantity of information required for regulatory compliance motivated progressive transportation companies to improve data processing techniques. Yellow Freight System was one of the first companies to be transformed by the computer age. In June, 1967, a separate Information Systems Department was created to deal with the data processing tasks, as well as other matters. This department collected, stored, and processed various types of information, some of which was used internally in the company. Certain reports processed here were for external use, such as the annual ICC reports. Payroll functions were a systems department task that expanded into a wide variety of data collection. The preparation of 7,500 paychecks was in itself a complicated problem. Driver pay presented the greatest difficulty since the factors considered in the pay calculations were exceptionally complex. In time, payroll forms included pertinent items for use by personnel, data for figuring maintenance expenses, and tax collection information. As the department expanded, it took on the function of collecting useful data for every department within the company.

Not only did the Information Systems Department collect, store, and process data, but it also eventually disseminated the data throughout the company. All of the terminals of the Yellow Freight System, Inc. were tied to the general office in Kansas City and were linked by a newly installed teleprocessing communications system. This system, with its message transmission and switching capability was a clear improvement over the teletype system formerly used. In addition, it provided for data entry to the computer. Freight bill information was transmitted to Yellow's terminals, and data from them collected in Kansas City, thus making them the company's primary source of information. A subsidiary computer system was developed for the direct entry of freight bill information to the inquiry tracing system. Capability to handle over 12,500 shipments per day on more than 5,000 trailers was originally provided. These facilities were expanded as increases in data warranted. From the information transmitted, the information services department planned to develop a shipment control system. Such a tracking system would make possible the establishment of a delivery service that could be reliable and guarantee punctual shipments.

The information services staff was in charge of the entire field of computer use and application. The department was housed in its own elaborate section of the general office building, and at the end of 1971 the communications system was IBM oriented, run on 512K Model 50, with backup and ancillary processing on a second model 50, which was also used for batch data processing. One hundred fifty communications terminals in over 100 Yellow locations were interconnected by a private, leased communications network. So vital to company operations were the computer facilities that a standby generating plant was installed in a newly constructed building nearby to ensure against interruption in the supply of electricity.

PLANNING AND ECONOMIC ANALYSIS

Of necessity a firm must engage in economic planning. In the early years these functions were a part of top management's thinking. But as the firm grew, management was forced to turn all its attention to the complex, as well as day-to-day, operations. Outside research organizations were utilized, but they proved only partially satisfactory. By the mid-1960's a full-time economist—later called economic analyst—had been hired. By 1969 the work of the economic analyst had become so important to the company that he was made a member of the planning group. He quickly became involved in two valuable and interesting projects: surveys of market and economic conditions in single cities and a ranking of the relative worth and merits of the 124 Standard Metropolitan Statistical Areas not served by Yellow Freight System. Some of the post-Watson-Wilson merger acquisitions can be traced to this study. For example, in 1970, Milwaukee was the largest area not served by Yellow. In 1971 an agreement to purchase Yule Truck Lines, which served Milwaukee, was reached. An example of a regional study was in New Haven, Conn. With the acquisition of New York & Worcester Express Co. in 1971 Yellow Freight System was brought into that market. The economic analyst also played a major role in the investigation of the terminal situation in the Los Angeles area. Thus far, the studies carried out have tended to relate to the economic conditions of a specific area and Yellow's potential there at the time of inquiry. Continued growth of the company will require economic forecasting.

The operational planning group was set up as a separate function in 1969 under the direction of one of Yellow Freight System's versatile and experienced vice-presidents. A staff of researchers and analysts was assembled. One of the first problems tackled was terminal and related pickups and delivery operations. At the new Baxter Springs, Kan., terminal started in 1971, over $1 million in automated freight handling equipment was installed. Other first priority projects in the group included load pattern studies and scheduling of line-haul runs.

After the recommendations of these studies were adopted productivity was increased, efficiency was improved, and top management was further convinced of the value of the group. Penetrating operational studies were also done to determine new terminal locations, and on the basis of these studies more terminals have been established.

The continuing expansion of Yellow created a need for a systematic and long-range planning activity free from the pressures of line responsibility. Top management solved this growth problem by creating the operational planning group. The workable solution was typical of those at Yellow Freight System.

14 / Management by Logic

The transformation of the Yellow Cab Transit Company from an Oklahoma City bus operation into the Yellow Freight System required 40 years of effort. This final chapter will discuss the group under whose leadership and direction the company prospered.

LEADERSHIP

From the early 1950's until 1968, at the time of the merger of Watson-Wilson Transportation System with Yellow Freight System, the board of directors had consisted of seven people elected each year at the annual meeting. During 1967, Gilbert C. Swanson, the former principal shareholder of Watson-Wilson, replaced R. L. Wagner, a director since 1964. Following Swanson's death in 1968, John S. Bransford, vice-president of Bransford, Sharp and Co., Insurance Brokers at Nashville, was elected a director. Bransford had been associated with the former Wilson Truck Company since the mid-1950's. Later in 1968 when the board was increased to nine members, Mark D. Robeson, executive vice-president of the company, and Cecil A. Johnson, a practicing attorney and general counsel of Swanson Enterprises of Omaha, were elected directors. The board was composed of these three, two directors (Donald L. McMorris and Professor L. L. Waters), elected in the early 1960's, plus four veteran directors first elected in

1952: Lester H. Brickman, Kenneth E. Midgley, George E. Powell, Sr., and George E. Powell, Jr. The board of directors has been the policy formulating body and general overseer of funds of the company.

Operations of the company, of course, have been performed by the working force; in very large measure the success of Yellow Freight System, Inc. could be attributed to its employees. Guiding the employees was the top management group, which was expanded in July, 1965, by the election of six additional vice-presidents: Harold H. Edwards, vice-president and treasurer; Burl Cotton, vice-president, terminals; V. Ray Alderson, vice-president, transportation; L. E. Tomlinson, vice-president, traffic; Lloyd C. Brandt, vice-president, sales; and Connie E. Hale, vice-president, insurance and safety. Significantly, each of these six new vice-presidents had been at Yellow Freight System more than ten years. During the following five years some new officers were elected and some departed. In 1967 Connie E. Hale left the company, and veteran vice-president William R. Riley, who had joined Yellow with the management change of 1952, established his own business.

In mid-1968 several executive changes were approved by the board of directors. After 16 years of service George E. Powell, Sr. was named honorary chairman of the board of directors. More than any other individual, he was responsible for the eminent position Yellow Freight System has attained in the transportation industry. George E. Powell, Jr., who remained chief executive officer, was elected chairman of the board. Donald L. McMorris succeeded to the presidency and became chief operating officer. Senior vice-president Mark D. Robeson became executive vice-president in charge of the administrative services department, which included the responsibility for legal, safety, insurance, regulatory compliance, personnel, and management development functions.

Yellow Freight had in the past shifted its top management people to various positions in order to familiarize them with the wide range of managerial functions in a trucking company. This policy proved satisfactory, and on Feb. 1, 1971, another series of executive changes were announced. The continuing officers after the Feb. 1 alterations were as follows: George E. Powell, Jr., chairman of the board; Donald L. McMorris, president; Mark D. Robeson, executive vice-president; Burl Cotton, group vice-president; V. Ray Alderson, vice-president, planning; Lloyd C. Brandt, vice-president, sales; Harold H. Edwards, vice-president, finance; Stephen P. Murphy, vice-president and assistant secretary; David D. Padgett, vice-president, properties; L. E. Tomlin-

Donald L. McMorris   Mark D. Robeson

son, vice-president, traffic; Kenneth E. Medgley, secretary and general
counsel; John M. Records, assistant secretary; and Raymond A.
Stewart, Jr., treasurer. The newly elected officers were as follows:
Robert E. Cowles, vice-president eastern central division; William F.
Hott, vice-president eastern division; Dale Merriman, vice-president
special hauling division; B. D. Pinkham, vice-president southwestern
division; Gerald C. R. Wheatley, assistant vice-president; Phillip A.
Spangler, assistant treasurer; and John R. Murphy, Jr., assistant secretary. Cowles, who joined Yellow in 1952, managed the company's first
area terminal at Marshall, Mich. Hott became a Yellow employee in
1963 and was instrumental in making the former Norwalk territory a
profitable region. Merriman joined Yellow in 1960, and he was
promoted to vice-president in recognition of his able work as general
manager of the special hauling division. Pinkham, who affiliated with
Yellow in 1956, was a strong force in the development of the west and
southwest after the Watson-Wilson take-over. Wheatley came to Yellow
Freight System from Midwest Research Institute in 1967 and was made
director of information services, the group he continued to head.
Spangler, a CPA, had been manager of terminal accounting since coming to Yellow in 1968. Murphy came to the company in 1970 from a
Kansas City law firm.

The management of Yellow Freight System, Inc. has traditionally served on the boards of other companies and associations. Several of Yellow's top people have accepted positions of leadership in a variety of organizations. Dr. Jack J. Holder, Jr., director of management development, was elected to the board of Johnson County Community College. Vice-president Harold E. Edwards has been president and chairman of the National Accounting and Finance Council of the American Trucking Association and president of the Transport Clearing House, Inc. of Kansas City. Chairman George E. Powell, Jr. has been a member of the board of banks and manufacturing companies and a trustee of the Kansas City Art Institute, the Midwest Research Institute, the Pembroke County Day School in Kansas City, and the Leelanau School at Glen Arbor, Michigan. President McMorris, a bank director, has also served on the board of United Campaign, Inc. of Greater Kansas City. The contributions of Mark Robeson alone are considerable: chairman, Western Highway Institute; regional director, Office of Emergency Transportation; chairman, Kansas Economic Development Commission; president, Kansas Motor Carriers Association; member, Urban Transportation Advisory Council of the Department of Transportation; director, National Safety Council; trustee, American Trucking Association-Foundation; a member of the executive committee, Highway Users Federation; director, Transportation Association of America; and in 1969, president of the American Trucking Association.

THE PROFIT PICTURE

The ultimate test of managerial prowess in any business organization is the earnings record. Yellow Freight System and its predecessor companies had a successful 20 year period from 1924 to 1944. From 1944 to 1952 earnings fell, and the company was for a short time in bad financial straits. During the next stage of the company's growth, from 1952 to 1970, the financial picture greatly improved, and the earnings record for this period is remarkable, as is illustrated in Table 14.

The 3,500,000 shares outstanding at the end of 1970 were the result of a 5 for 2 stock dividend voted by the board of directors on Jan. 24, 1969. Following ICC approval, shareholders of record as of March 28 benefited from the split, which occurred on April 9. At the annual meeting in April, 1969, shareholders voted approval of an increase

TABLE 14
Revenues and Earnings for Yellow Freight
System, Inc., 1954–1970

	Revenues*	Assets*	Net Income*	Earnings Per Share†
1954	$ 8.6	$ 3.7	$0.1	$0.04
1955	10.3	8.4	0.3	0.10
1956	12.4	9.7	0.5	0.14
1957	18.0	14.5	0.4	0.11
1958	25.0	14.6	0.6	0.18
1959	31.3	18.9	0.9	0.27
1960	32.0	16.5	0.5	0.14
1961	27.3	14.2	0.7	0.20
1962	29.7	15.2	1.6	0.47
1963	35.5	17.5	2.5	0.72
1964	42.6	22.7	3.2	0.91
1965	83.6	50.7	3.3	0.95
1966	104.6	54.3	5.3	1.50
1967	104.2	60.8	4.5	1.29
1968	132.7	72.4	7.0	2.01
1969	161.7	91.9	7.0	2.01
1970	170.3	101.8	7.2	2.05

*In millions of dollars.
†Earnings per share calculated on the basis of 3,500,000 shares outstanding, Dec. 31, 1970.
SOURCE: Annual reports to stockholders, 1959 to 1970, and company financial reports for previous years.

in the company's authorized capital stock from 3,500,000 to 10,000,000 common shares. At the time immediate issuance of additional shares was not contemplated. The action provided the opportunity for the company to have shares available should an attractive use appear at some future date.

Balanced growth had been a management goal for some years. The growth in both revenues and earnings can be seen from the data in Table 14. By 1966 operating revenues were large enough that Yellow, ranking forty-eighth, joined the *Fortune* list of the 50 largest transportation companies. In the growth rate of earnings per share Yellow ranked fifth, and in net income as a per cent of invested capital Yellow's position was fourth. In 1967 Yellow was forty-seventh in size, sixth in the rate of earnings per share, and ninth in net income as a per cent of invested capital. In 1968 Yellow was fortieth, fourth, and first in the respective positions; in 1969, Yellow was thirty-second, third and third. By 1970, Yellow ranked thirty-first, fourth, and third, respectively, and the July, 1971 issue of *Fortune* even featured the article "Golden Profits at Yellow Freight."

YELLOW STAYS IN MOTION

Each year top management of Yellow Freight System has met in a retreat location in order to discuss long-range planning. One of the goals frequently mentioned at these meetings was continued growth. Through small acquisitions that augmented the company's authority and through more intensive coverage of the operating area, this goal has been well met. A second objective, staying in the transportation industry, has also received attention through the years and careful consideration at each long-range planning meeting. This goal has likewise been successfully achieved. As with other motor carriers, the large geographic coverage and vast number of customers from all industries naturally diversified Yellow Freight System's activities. In a study of 29 publically held carriers of general freight Yellow was one of five truck lines receiving revenues from other than straight motor carrier operations. But Yellow was the only company also engaged in freight forwarding.[1] The success of Yellow Freight System in both areas was uncommon, as the *Fortune* rankings indicated. Yellow was one of eight trucking common carriers included in the 1970 list of 50 transportation companies.

Business leaders have long directed their attention to problems outside the business community. For instance, the common carrier industry for years has been involved in safety and highway protection legislation. Because demands for truck transport have increased, the trucking industry has taken a stand on the use of taxes collected for highway construction: the taxes should be used specifically for that purpose. Air pollution has become a major concern, and Yellow has contributed to cleaner diesel engines by providing data based on the company's experience as a nation-wide trucker to engine manufacturers.

Yellow Freight management has also continually improved and made the working environment more pleasant at the company terminals. The terminals have often been unique for landscaping and attractive architecture. At the St. Louis terminal a 12-foot high outdoor sculpture was installed. The work was created by a student at the Kansas City Art Institute from an aluminum wing tank from a junked military aircraft. The company commissioned the recycling of the wing into a piece of sculpture in keeping with its long-standing policy of adding works of art to the communities it served.

---

[1]Robert W. Burdick, "A Study of Diversification in the Motor Carrier Industry," *Transportation Journal* (Summer, 1970), pp. 16-32.

The national business conditions have affected Yellow, as well as other trucking companies. The problem of inflation concerned Yellow's management because trucking joined other industries in the cost-price squeeze. The regulatory lag in transportation company operations added an extra burden. More efficient equipment, capable of carrying greater payloads, could help increase productivity. However, size and weight restrictions in certain states have prevented the complete introduction of such equipment. Yellow's management has been working with legislative bodies to make certain that all the relevant facts are known. These examples serve to indicate that the variety and extent of management challenges can only be expected to increase.

An often cited business tenet is that a company is only as good as its management. In discussing the future of a company, therefore, management prowess takes on even greater significance. Prognostications of revenue growth, capital and personnel investment, goals, standards, and performance levels can all be determined, both for the company as a whole and for the various divisions of the company. Yet, all of these items together are less meaningful predictors of success than is the record of management achievement, which is the real key to the future of the company. If the past is prologue, the chances for continued progress for Yellow Freight System are indeed bright.

The emphasis of this study has been on the approaches and tactics of Yellow's management throughout the years of the company. A. J. Harrell started in a small way in Oklahoma City in the early 1920's. Through hard work and wise decisions he built a truckline, which established a profit record of phenomenal heights during the 1930's— the period of the greatest depression in American economic history. Houston, Dallas, San Antonio, Oklahoma City, Tulsa, and Amarillo were small outposts compared to the cities of the North and East, but they grew and increasingly required the goods that Yellow could haul to them. Houston's population grew from 138,276 in 1920 to 384,512 in 1940; Dallas, 158,976 to 294,734; San Antonio, 161,379 to 253,854; Oklahoma City, 91,295 to 204,424; Tulsa, 72,075 to 142,157; and Amarillo, 15,494 to 51,686. By 1940 Chicago was past 3 million, Detroit above 1.5 million, and St. Louis and Cleveland had exceeded 800,000. Careful expansion developed the Yellow Transit company from an Oklahoma City-Tulsa carrier into an extensive truckline from Chicago and Louisville to Houston, San Antonio, and Amarillo.

By 1944 Harrell was ready to sell, and the ownership and direction of Yellow Transit were moved to New York City. The area served by the company continued to grow. After World War II and during the

Korean conflict the trucking industry enjoyed enormous growth, but Yellow Transit failed to make the grade. It was quite an ironic change for a company that had made financial history during the Great Depression to enter bankruptcy during a boom period of the trucking industry. But the aims of management had changed, and personal goals interfered with company objectives. The entanglement of Yellow Transit and its 48 subsidiaries was, at best, a legal nightmare.

In late 1952 George Powell, Sr. gathered a fresh management team and set out to straighten Yellow. Policies recalling the days of A. J. Harrell were combined with the modern know-how of the 1950's and 1960's. Decisions based on sound business logic made trucking history. The entire fleet of rolling stock was modernized at one time. A new concept in terminals—the *area terminal*—was developed. Michigan Motor Freight Lines, in some ways equal in size to Yellow Transit itself, was merged into the company. Experimentation with short-haul traffic, although logically and forcefully approached, proved unsuccessful. A forwarding company was added to the Yellow Transit Freight Lines family and led to the creation of the Yellow Freight System. Controlling interest in the Watson-Wilson Transportation System, Inc., a coast-to-coast carrier, was acquired and the merger consummated in 1968. In 1969 certain operating rights of the Norwalk subsidiaries of United-Buckingham Freight Lines were purchased. The area from Washington, D.C., to Boston to Cleveland was added to the service area. Several smaller authorities became part of Yellow. By 1970 the company was the third largest truck line and thirty-first largest transportation company in the country when measured by operating revenues. That year about 8,000 people were employees of Yellow Freight System.

Throughout the years since 1952 the managerial decisions have been based on conclusions drawn from the experience and knowledge of the entire executive staff. Perhaps the single greatest factor in the success of Yellow Freight System has been the skill with which human assets have been employed. The worker has been treated first as a person and second as an employee. People with ideas have made the difference.

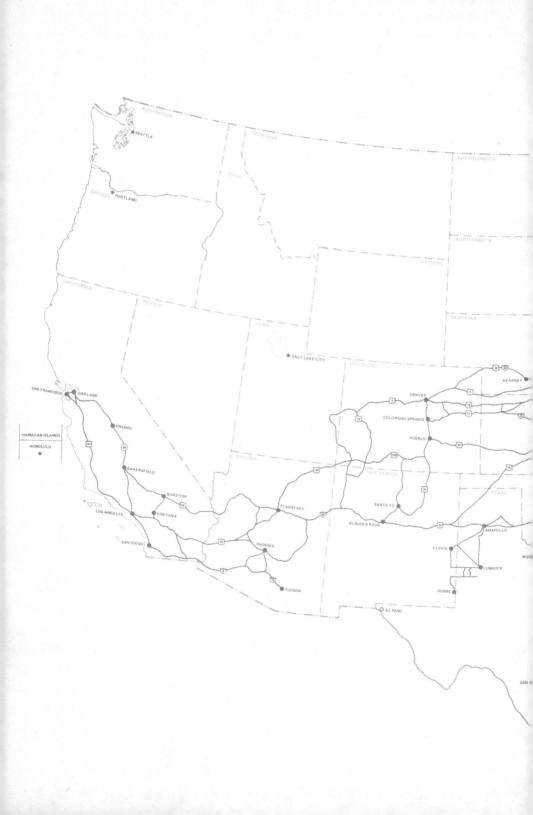